SYDNEYFOOD

For Natalie

With big thanks to: Catie and Neale for asking me to do this book; Vanessa and Natalie for their commitment and patience; Elsa, Michelle and Valli for their great talent and hard work; Jody for her professionalism and rigorous testing; everyone at bills and bills2 who allowed me to take the time to do this book, especially Kylie, Cassie and Amanda, and to all my loyal customers who have supported bills and bills2 over the years; the following suppliers for produce: the freshest seafood from Demcos (and the scary live marrons), wonderful fruit and vegetables from BJ Lizard, meat from Vics Meats, salmon from Mohr Foods and bread from Victoire. And finally Mum, Dad and Alan for their tireless support of me and the businesses over the years.

The publisher would like to thank the following for their generosity in supplying props for the book: Bison Homewares, Orrefors Kosta Boda, Ordal Australia, Empire Homewares, Orson and Blake, White, Space Furniture, Major and Tom, Verosol, Spence and Lyda, Jarass Imports, Shack, Funkis Swedish Forms. Thanks also to: Waverley Council, Sydney Morning Herald Good Living Growers Markets Pyrmont, Royal Botanic Gardens Sydney, Sydney Fish Markets, Sydney Opera House Trust

Published by Murdoch Books®, a division of Murdoch Magazines Pty Ltd, GPO Box 1203, Sydney NSW 2001

Project Manager: Anna Waddington; Art Director: Vanessa Holden; Photographer: Elsa Hutton; Additional photography [pp. 59, 73, 86, 169]:Tony Lyon; Additional photography [pp. 3 (images 1, 4, 5), 4, 5, 18-20, 68-70, 128-130, back cover (images 1, 3 , 4)]: Con Poulos; Editor: Natalie Filatoff; International Editor: Neale Whitaker; Food Editor: Jody Vassallo; Food Stylist: Michelle Noerianto; Home Economist: Valli Little; Recipe Testing: Ben Masters, Ross Dobson, Valli Little, Jody Vassallo; Props: Trish Heagerty

Chief Executive: Juliet Rogers; Publisher: Kay Scarlett

National Library of Australia Cataloguing-in-Publication Data
Granger, Bill (William). Sydney Food. ISBN 0 86411 991 7.
Cookery - New South Wales - Sydney. 2. Restaurateurs - New South Wales
Sydney. I. Title. 641.5099441

Distributed in the United Kingdom by Macmillan, Houndmills, Basingstoke, Hampshire, RG21 6XS, ph (0) 1256 329242

S Y D N E Y F O O D

B I L L   G R A N G E R

MURDOCH
B O O K S

CONTENTS

BILLS

I've always liked to cook, but moving to Sydney as an art student changed my perception of what food can be. I've always enjoyed food that's fresh and light, that boosts your energy rather than absorbing it; in 1988 Sydney already had the ingredients, and the chefs, like Neil Perry, who were bringing them to life. My father was a butcher. When I moved to Sydney from Melbourne, I discovered fish.

Like a lot of students, I worked as a waiter. In my case it was at La Passion du Fruit (then in Paddington, it's now in Surry Hills). The owner, Christine Juillet, only served French-Mediterranean-style breakfasts and lunch at Passion, and agreed to let me open for dinner three nights a week. Passion just had what was called a 'tearoom' license, which meant we weren't allowed to cook on the premises.

work, staff from nearby St Vincents Hospital on their lunch break, lone Saturday brunchers – all bump elbows over the papers and magazines at the big table.

When I went to San Francisco, in 1989, I ate at China Moon, Barbara Tropp's famous restaurant. It was the first time I'd tasted Asian food cooked in a modern way and it blew my mind. I bought her book, 'The Modern Art of Chinese Cooking' and the vital, elegant flavours of that food became a big part of bills and bills2 (which I opened in 1996). And when Kylie Kwong, who had worked with Neil Perry to make Sydney's famous Rockpool restaurant a success, decided to start a restaurant of her own, she came to work with me while the new venture was in the planning stages. We got along so well – we both love Chinese peasant

BUSINESS PEOPLE ON THEIR WAY TO WORK, STAFF FROM NEARBY ST VINCENTS HOSPITAL ON THEIR LUNCH BREAK, LONE SATURDAY BRUNCHERS - ALL BUMP ELBOWS OVER THE PAPERS AND MAGAZINES AT THE BIG TABLE.

I did all the cooking that my venture required at my mother's place in Darling Point, and then assembled the dishes (reheating soup in a coffee pot, steaming asparagus in an electric kettle) at the restaurant. Much of what I made was fresh. Chrissie's influence, and that quirk of restaurant law, taught me how to combine the best produce I could find, with elements I had pre-prepared, into dishes people enjoyed – this is what a lot of Sydneysiders do at home in their kitchens.

I've always been inspired by the domestic, the kitchen table as the heart of the household. When I opened bills, in 1993, it had council restrictions that allowed us to seat only 35 people at a time. I put in the big communal table to fill the space in an inviting way. It turned out to be what Sydneysiders wanted. Business people on their way to

food – that we decided to go into business together, opening 'Billy Kwong'.

At home, food has to be simple and virtually instant. I often combine something prepared in the commercial kitchens at work with more fresh ingredients. Interestingly, I think that's what most Sydneysiders do. This book combines the favourite recipes from our menus over the years, with ideas for simplifying them, tips on where to buy readymade specialties and, hopefully, the inspiration for how you might assemble them. It has in it the essence of my love for Sydney's adventurous food culture.

I hope it brings you to the table in a relaxed and enthusiastic way.

Bill

MARKET FRESH

First light, Sydney Morning Herald Good Living
Growers Market, Pyrmont

THE RAW PRAWN

Snap-frozen on the trawler, or fresh from the sea, green prawns let you decide how they'll taste. Boil them until they turn rich orange-pink, in a pot of salted water with a few slices of lemon and a handful of parsley, then serve with lime or coriander mayonnaise; or marinate them in olive oil, lemon juice and chopped chilli or garlic before barbecuing with their shells on.

COOKED FARM TIGER PRAWNS $24·50

SEAFOOD

SUN ON THE BOARDWALK, PELICANS CRUISING THE PYLONS, A SHIMMERING ABUNDANCE OF SEAFOOD. SYDNEY FISHMARKET CAN SATISFY A CROWD.

SEAFOOD PLATTER is a term to strike fear into the palate. Even professional chefs often take the idea over-board with batter and shrill sauces. But the notion is seductive – a selection of the best you can buy, simply prepared and plattered, each variety of fish and shellfish on its own, antipasti-style, with a green salad, a bowl of lemon or lime wedges and crusty bread.

COOKED MUD CRAB 8. 50

Start with the intention to poach a fish. A whole Tasmanian salmon takes on the flavours of court bouillon: a cup of dry white wine, a tablespoon of salt, two chopped sticks of celery, two chopped carrots, two onions (quartered), half a bunch of parsley and enough water to raise the liquid to cover the fish. Bring these ingredients to the boil in a pan long enough to hold the fish. Add the salmon, return to the boil, remove from heat, cover and allow to stand for 30 minutes. Remove the fish from the pan, peel off the skin and serve whole with herb mayonnaise.

If the market has clear, wobbly scallops on the shell, grill up a stack. They cook quickly with a little olive oil, salt and pepper.

Barbecued scampi make a spectacular platter. Halve them down the spine, don't rinse, just brush with garlic oil, season with salt and pepper and cook flesh-side-down on a hot, oiled barbecue grill or plate. Serve with fennel and chilli relish (see page 163).

IN SEASON

Summer Atlantic salmon, blue swimmer crab, flathead, flounder, leather jacket, West Australian marron, Moreton Bay bugs, mussels, prawns (bay, endeavour, king and school), sardines, scallops, snapper, sweetlip emperor, yabbies.

Autumn Atlantic salmon, barramundi, crabs (blue swimmer and mud crab), eel, flathead, Moreton Bay bugs, mullet, mussels, prawns (banana, king and tiger), shark, squid.

Winter barramundi, blue grenadier, King George whiting, ling, Murray cod, pearl perch, red emperor, school whiting, tailor, tiger prawns, tuna.

Spring Atlantic salmon, coral trout, flathead, King George whiting, mussels, ocean trout, prawns (bay, school and tiger), redfish, scallops, spanner crab.

URBAN LIVING

URBANITES SQUEEZE SHOPPING INTO SMALL HOURS AND PLASTIC BAGS. A DISCERNING MARKET, SYDNEYSIDERS' NEEDS ARE MET IN FRESH AND TRADITIONAL WAYS.

ON THE PLAZA

The fruit barrows of Sydney's CBD may have become kiosks, but in kerb-side style the "barrowmen" of Circular Quay, Martin Place and Town Hall will still give you an extra apple for a friendly smile, or strike bargains at the end of the day to clear their stock. An avocado, a lemon, a ripe tomato and a crusty roll from a café, makes an easy office lunch. Ten nectarines bought at the start of the week fill a bowl on your desk to satisfy sugar cravings. Friday-night commuters do a deal on mangoes for daiquiris – the fragrance of a bag of ripe fruit is enough to transport a group of elbow-to-elbow train passengers bound for the suburbs.

GROWERS MARKET
The Sydney Morning Herald Good Living Growers Market is more an open-air gourmet supermarket, and reflects the varied produce – freshly harvested, bottled, stuffed in sausage skins, baked, fermented, sprouted, plucked and pickled – of the state of New South Wales. Get there early, say 7.30 am, start with a cup of freshly roasted and brewed, locally grown coffee and move on to fill your basket with bundles of fresh rhubarb, organically grown new potatoes, a plump free-range chicken, a little pail of fresh goats cheese, a wholemeal loaf studded with sunflower seeds. The market appears on the first Saturday of each month, a tented settlement on the Pyrmont shore of Sydney Harbour.

IN STOCK

The gourmet superstore does bread, cheese, classy condiments and fruit jellies; or was that creamy feta, a crash course in olives, tins of vine leaves and rosewater Turkish delight? From those that gift wrap to the MFC where hookas hang from the ceiling, check our list on page 189 for culinary one-stop shops.

PRE-PREPPED

Vacuum-packed gnocchi, ready to simmer, drizzle with herb butter and sprinkle with grated Parmesan. Jars of spice-rich curry pastes to get dinner started. Meats rolled around fillings or marinated by the butcher, ready to bake or stir fry, just add fresh vegetables. Pre-prepped foods lighten the load of cooking on a lightning-flash schedule. Pizza bases are a hotbed of creativity – lavish with caramelised onion, criss-cross with anchovies and dot with black olives before baking. A can of hummus from Lebanon just needs a little extra lemon juice, some chopped parsley and a sprinkling of sumac before serving with oven-warmed Turkish bread. Take what's on offer to ease your path through the day.

DISH UP

Supermarkets like Thai-Kee have inexpensive utensil and china sections to set up for a comfortable life: steamers for cooking dumplings bought at Chinese Noodle Restaurant or a whole snapper with ginger and shallots; big sculptural wire draining spoons for scooping tempura vegetables; blue- and white bowls in all sizes, which turn crisp against plain white linens and platters; woks for quick cooking; clay pots for broth-based simmering; and chopsticks for digging in.

ASIAN FLAVOUR

CLEAN GREENS, NOURISHING NOODLES, MEAT OFF THE HOOK. ASIA HAS ADDED LINKS TO SYDNEY'S FOOD CHAIN THAT TIE US TO OUR NEIGHBOURS MORE FUNDAMENTALLY THAN DIPLOMACY.

WING BEANS + WATER LILIES

You'll find Thai, Chinese and Vietnamese green-grocers like fragrant islands half submerged amongst Sydney's suburban sprawl. At Pontip, waterlilies are sold for the culinary value of their long coiled stems: slice them from the flower (which can then float in a bowl as table decoration), peel like rhubarb, cut on the diagonal into bite-sized segments, and add to prawn curry just before serving. Or toss the segments in a wok with hot oil, finely chopped chilli and garlic before adding to chicken noodle soup (see page 87). Papaya, when it's unripe, is another Asian green: julienne or grate it to make a crunchy salad base (see page 107) that goes well with barbecued meat or shellfish. Thai basil has the taste of aniseed and cloves – use it sparingly, sliced very finely, to give bite to coconut-creamy dishes. Wing beans add visual appeal to steamed vegetable combinations: blanch and slice before tossing with a dressing made of fish sauce, lime juice, palm sugar (dissolved in a little hot water) and chopped chilli.

GREAT LENGTHS

From fat flaccid coils of resting dough, the noodle maker teases and tears slim elastic lengths. Watch the chef at work in the kitchen of the Chinese Noodle Restaurant while getting your chopsticks around some of his handmade dumplings. For fresh noodles to cook at home, stroll through the food-redolent streets of Chinatown to Thai-Kee Supermarket. Slippery broad ribbons of rice noodle take barely two minutes to heat in boiling water: toss them with freshly steamed mussels in the shell and a dressing of fish sauce, lime juice, chilli and vegetable oil, then sprinkle with chopped coriander. Spaghetti-like egg noodles are great with Chinese roast pork, dressed with soy sauce and sesame oil and served with steamed vegetables.

BARBECUE SHAPES

They hang in the windows, glossy and tanned with spice and glaze. One renowned purveyor of barbecued meats is Emperors Garden BBQ and Noodles in Sydney's Chinatown. Quail, suckling pork and succulent duck – takeaway to make your own. Shredded duck flesh and skin makes a superb salad: toss it with finely shredded cabbage, fresh bean sprouts and a dressing made from hoisin sauce, black vinegar, lime juice and sesame oil; sprinkle with toasted sesame seeds before serving with bowls of fragrant rice. The quail only needs lemon juice and Szechuan pepper-and-salt (in a small pan, over low heat, dry roast two tablespoons of sea salt and a teaspoon of szechuan pepper berries; grind and store in jar); serve it with wok-tossed Chinese greens. Shred the pork, roll in a rice paper wrapper with spring onion, and dip in chilli sauce (see note, page 148).

THE COMMON WEALTH

Like grated Parmesan, Italian food is sprinkled all over Sydney, with varying degrees of authenticity. Pizza, pasta and focaccia have been adopted and adapted; from the cheesy grin of franchises, to the zampone (stuffed pigs trotters) of a restaurant like L'ucciola in Balmain, the range of Italian experience can satisfy every appetite. For people cooking at home, some of the best ingredients come from the Leichhardt-Haberfield area. The sausages of AC Butchery can bring accolades to every barbecue chef. Haberfield Bakery often sells out of its chewy, crusty, fragrant loaves. Pasticceria Papa and A & P Sulfaro offer custard-filled Italian pastries, home-made gelati and ice creams that call into question your intentions to cook dessert. Take home cantucci, Tuscan almond biscuits, for dipping in glasses of Vin Santo (Italian dessert wine) – an intoxicating end to Italianate evenings.

ITALIAN INFLUENCE

WALKING DOWN THE AISLE WITH A CAN OF PEELED TOMATOES WAS ONCE AS 'ETHNIC' AS SYDNEY FOOD SHOPPING DARED TO BE. NOW WE'RE WEDDED TO THE MED, BUT OUR FIRST LOVE IS STILL ITALY.

DEEP SPICE
Herbs used to be dried and stored to death in sets of little matching jars. Now the pendulum has swung and our knowledge of fresh herbs has almost over-powered our hunger to know about the flavours of dried spice. Mediterranean countries combine the spices that add heat and richness, pungency and sweet warmth to dishes of meat, grains and vegetables. One local source of ingredients and know-how is Herbies Spices (see page 189).

Fresh ricotta from Paesanella Brothers (left) is just made to be spread on Haberfield Bakery bread (above).

16

CAN OPENER

There is no substitute for canned tomatoes. When you need reliable, deep-flavoured juiciness and instant, peeled tenderness, the can has the goods. Canned tomatoes cook down rapidly into a sauce to spoon over fresh spinach or herb pasta from Pastabilities (below); enrich a soup; sop into an Italian bread salad with olives and chopped basil; and decorate a shelf with a line of labels that seem to leap at you from an old Sophia Loren movie.

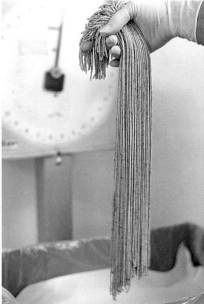

BREAKFAST

First dip, Bondi Icebergs Pool,
Bondi Beach

PAPAYA WAKES THE PALATE

COFFEE KICKSTARTS THE BRAIN. YOUR KEY TURNS IN THE IGNITION, THE SUNROOF SLIDES BACK AND SYDNEY GETS ON ITS WAY. WORKDAY MORNINGS ARE SERIOUS WITH CEREALS AND THE TASTE TWIST OF SHEEPS MILK YOGHURT, OR A FIVE-GRAIN PORRIDGE SIMMERING WHILE THE SHOWER STEAMS. WEEKENDS WATCH BREAKERS ROLL INTO THE BEACH AS BUTTER SIZZLES IN THE PAN AND RICOTTA PANCAKES ARE THE ONLY ONES TO FLIP. WALK AROUND THE HEADLAND WITH A GOLDEN DELICIOUS APPLE IN YOUR POCKET, STOPPING TO BUY THE PAPERS AND RICH RATIONS OF BACON. TOAST IS A HOME FRAGRANCE WITH SUBTLE VARIATIONS – CHEWY SOURDOUGH, YEASTY PIDE, OR QUINTON'S FIG-AND-CASHEW-STUDDED LOAF.

RICOTTA HOTCAKES WITH HONEYCOMB BUTTER

Born in America, the hotcake has assimilated well into Australian breakfast society. Take it back to its roots by substituting maple syrup for the gold-flecked crunch-sensation butter.

At bills we use a fresh ricotta from Paesanella... and I've been known to make the butter with chocolate-coated honeycomb in moments of decadence.

1¹/3 cups ricotta
3/4 cup (6 fl oz) milk
4 eggs, separated
1 cup plain (all-purpose) flour
1 teaspoon baking powder
a pinch of salt
50 g (1¹/2 oz) butter

to serve
banana
honeycomb butter, sliced (below)
icing (confectioners') sugar for dusting

Place ricotta, milk and egg yolks in a mixing bowl and mix to combine.

Sift the flour, baking powder and salt into a bowl. Add to the ricotta mixture and mix until just combined.

Place egg whites in a clean dry bowl and beat until stiff peaks form. Fold egg whites through batter in two batches, with a large metal spoon.

Lightly grease a large non-stick frying pan with a small portion of the butter and drop 2 tablespoons of batter per hotcake into the pan (don't cook more than 3 per batch). Cook over low to medium heat for 2 minutes, or until hotcakes have golden undersides. Turn hotcakes and cook on the other side until golden and cooked through. Transfer to a plate and quickly assemble with other ingredients.

Slice one banana lengthways onto a plate, stack 3 hotcakes on top with a slice of honeycomb butter. Dust with icing sugar. Serves 6–8.

note Hotcake batter can be stored for up to 24 hours, covered with plastic wrap in the refrigerator.

HONEYCOMB BUTTER

250 g (8 oz) unsalted butter, softened
100 g (3¹/3 oz) sugar honeycomb, crushed with a rolling pin
2 tablespoons honey

Place all ingredients in a food processor and blend until smooth. Shape into a log on plastic wrap, roll, seal and chill in a refrigerator for 2 hours. Store leftover honeycomb butter in the freezer – it's great on toast.

At a pinch, you need only marinate the tomatoes for a few minutes.

PAN-TOASTED SANDWICH WITH TOMATO AND FONTINA

Perfect hangover food as devised by Harry's Bar in Venice. Substitute any white cheese for the fontina. Add rocket or prosciutto. Make a mini version to serve with drinks (pre-hangover food), wrapped with a twist of greaseproof paper for easy handling.

100 ml (3^1/$_3$ fl oz) extra virgin olive oil
4 cloves garlic, chopped
1 red chilli, chopped
1 teaspoon sea salt
freshly ground black pepper
4 tomatoes, cut into ^{1}/$_2$ cm thick slices
8 large thick slices wholemeal bread
75 g (2^1/$_2$ oz) fontina cheese, finely sliced
16 basil leaves, plus extra to serve
50 g (1^1/$_2$ oz) butter

Place olive oil, garlic, chilli, salt and pepper in a large shallow dish and mix well. Add the sliced tomatoes and marinate for 2 hours. Brush one side of each slice of bread with some of the olive oil from the tomatoes. Place the cheese evenly on top of half the bread slices, on the oiled sides. Top with basil leaves, tomatoes and a second slice of bread, oil side down.

Melt half the butter in large frying pan over medium heat and add 2 sandwiches. Cover with a plate and weigh down with a can. Cook sandwiches until golden brown on each side. Cook the remaining sandwiches. Serve hot with extra basil leaves. Makes 4 sandwiches.

Really, any fruit is great in this recipe. One of my favourite combinations is mango and passionfruit.

FRESH BIRCHER MUESLI WITH STONE FRUIT

A little bit Heidi, a little bit Bondi. Oats are said to be a calming start to the day – the perfect prep for that job interview or marketing brainstorm meeting. In winter, do it with plump, soaked raisins and pears.

2 cups rolled oats
1 cup (8 fl oz) apple juice
1 cup coarsely grated apple
1/2 cup natural yoghurt
juice of 1 lemon
1/2 cup sliced peaches and nectarines
1/4 cup mixed berries
2 tablespoons honey

Place oats and apple juice in a bowl and soak for 1 hour, or overnight. Add grated apple, yoghurt and lemon juice to oat mixture and mix well. Spoon into serving bowls and top with fruit. Drizzle with honey. Serves 4.

SWEETCORN FRITTERS WITH ROAST TOMATO AND BACON

Corn off the cob is essential to give texture and a fresh edge to these fritters. They're also delicious served with avocado salsa; or in mini form, as a base for smoked salmon and crème fraîche, to be enjoyed with drinks.

1 cup plain (all-purpose) flour
1 teaspoon baking powder
1/4 teaspoon salt
1/4 teaspoon paprika
1 tablespoon sugar
2 eggs
1/2 cup (4 fl oz) milk
2 cups fresh corn kernels, cut from the cob
1/2 cup diced red capsicum (pepper)

1/2 cup sliced spring (green) onions
1/4 cup chopped coriander (cilantro) and parsley (combined)
4 tablespoons vegetable oil
to serve
8 halves roast tomatoes (below)
1 bunch rocket (arugula), washed and dried
4 rashers grilled bacon
olive oil

The fritter batter can be kept for up to 3 days, but do not mix the batter with the vegetables more than an hour before you're ready to cook, or the fritters will be soggy.

Sift flour, baking powder, salt and paprika into a large bowl, stir in sugar and make a well in the centre. In a separate bowl, combine eggs and milk. Gradually add the egg mixture to the dry ingredients and whisk until you have a smooth, lump-free batter. The batter will be quite stiff.

Place corn, capsicum, spring onions and herbs in a mixing bowl and add just enough batter to lightly bind them (about 3/4 cup). Heat 2 tablespoons vegetable oil in a non-stick frying pan on medium heat, then drop in 2 tablespoons of batter per fritter and cook 4 fritters at a time. Cook for 2 minutes, or until the underside of each fritter is golden. Turn over and cook fritters on the other side. Transfer to a plate and keep warm while cooking the remaining fritters.

to serve place one fritter on each plate and top each with two halves of roast tomato, a small handful of rocket and a rasher of grilled bacon. Finish with a second fritter and drizzle olive oil around the base of the stack. Serves 4.

ROAST TOMATOES

4 ripe Roma tomatoes, sliced in half lengthways
4 tablespoons extra virgin olive oil
sea salt
freshly ground black pepper

Preheat the oven to 180°C (350°F). Place tomatoes on a baking tray, cut-side-up, and drizzle with olive oil. Sprinkle liberally with sea salt and pepper. Roast in the oven for 40 minutes.

Coconut bread batter can be kept in the fridge for two days. Just pour into tins when you're ready and bake according to the recipe.

COCONUT BREAD

Marked "never to be replaced" on the menus at bills, this Jamaican bread is intended to be served with salt-fish relish. Lime marmalade goes well with it, too. Keep slices in the freezer for workdays when you'd rather be in the Caribbean.

2 eggs
300 ml (10 fl oz) milk
1 teaspoon vanilla essence
2¹/2 cups plain (all-purpose) flour
2 teaspoons baking powder
2 teaspoons cinnamon
1 cup caster (superfine) sugar
150 g (5 oz) shredded coconut
75 g (2¹/2 oz) unsalted butter, melted

to serve
butter
icing (confectioners') sugar

Preheat oven to 180°C (350°F). Lightly whisk eggs, milk and vanilla together.

Sift flour, baking powder and cinnamon into a bowl, add sugar and coconut, and stir to combine. Make a well in the centre and gradually stir in the egg mixture until just combined. Add melted butter and stir until the mixture is just smooth, being careful not to over-mix.

Pour into a greased and floured 21 x 10 cm (8¹/2 x 4 in) loaf tin and bake in the preheated oven for 1 hour, or until bread is cooked when tested with a skewer.

Leave in the tin to cool for 5 minutes, and remove to cool further on a wire rack. Serve in thick slices, toasted, buttered and dusted with icing sugar. Makes 8–10 thick slices.

CHOCOLATE WAFFLES WITH CHERRY COMPOTE AND VANILLA YOGHURT

Chocolate lovers consider this the ultimate start to the day. To finish the day, you can make it again as a dessert, served with cherries macerated in liqueur and honey, and crème fraîche instead of the yoghurt.

3 eggs, separated
1½ cups (12 fl oz) milk
1 teaspoon vanilla essence
60 g (2 oz) unsalted butter, melted
100 g (3⅓ oz) good-quality dark chocolate, chopped
1½ cups plain (all-purpose) flour
2 teaspoons baking powder

a pinch of salt
to serve
cherry compote (below)
vanilla yoghurt (see page 41)
good-quality dark chocolate, shaved

Place egg yolks, milk, vanilla and melted butter in a bowl and stir until combined.

Place chocolate in a heatproof bowl resting over a saucepan of hot water over low heat and heat until chocolate has melted. Allow to cool slightly.

Sift flour, baking powder and salt into a bowl and make a well in the centre. Gradually stir in the milk mixture until the batter is smooth.

Place the egg whites in a clean dry bowl and beat until soft peaks form. Fold into the batter with a large metal spoon. Add the melted chocolate and swirl through the batter.

Cook according to the waffle-iron manufacturer's directions.

Serve with cherry compote, vanilla yoghurt and shaved chocolate. Serves 4.

CHERRY COMPOTE

½ cup caster (superfine) sugar
250 g (8 oz) frozen cherries
¼ teaspoon ground cinnamon

Place sugar in a small saucepan with ½ cup (4 fl oz) water over medium heat. Stir to dissolve, then boil until liquid is reduced by half. Add cherries and cinnamon and cook for 2 minutes. Remove from heat and cool before spooning over waffles.

JAM DOUGHNUTS

These classic, yeast-risen doughnuts take a fair amount of work, but they're worth it on a lazy Sunday. Serve them with good strong coffee, and a stack of absorbing newspapers.

1 cup (8 fl oz) warm water
2 x 7 g (1/4 oz) sachets dried yeast
31/2 tablespoons caster (superfine) sugar
220 g (7 oz) butter
5 eggs
1 teaspoon salt
450 g (14 oz) plain (all-purpose) flour

vegetable oil for deep-frying
1 cup caster (superfine) sugar
2 teaspoons ground cinnamon
raspberry jam

Place the water, yeast and 1 teaspoon sugar in a bowl and mix to combine. Leave in a warm place for 10 minutes or until foaming.

Beat the butter and remaining sugar until creamy. Add the eggs one at a time, beating after each addition. Add the yeast mixture, salt and flour and beat with a wooden spoon until smooth. Cover with plastic wrap and set aside to rise in a warm place for 11/2–2 hours or until doubled in volume. Punch down the dough, remove from the bowl, wrap in plastic wrap and refrigerate for 3 hours or overnight.

Turn half the dough onto a lightly floured surface and pat it out to a 3 cm (11/4 in) thickness. Using a 5 cm (2 in) round cutter, cut out rounds then roll these into balls. Repeat with the remaining dough.

Pour the oil into a deep saucepan or deep fryer to a depth of 6 cm (21/2 in). Heat to 175°C (335°F), or until a little of the dough dropped into the oil floats to the surface and browns. Fry the doughnuts in batches, being careful not to crowd them, until golden brown. Remove the puffed golden doughnuts with a slotted spoon and place on a wire rack to drain away any excess oil.

Combine the caster sugar and cinnamon on a sheet of baking paper and roll the warm doughnuts in the sugar to coat them. With a piping bag, pipe a little raspberry jam into the middle of each doughnut while warm. Serve immediately. Makes 16.

In summer I like to serve this porridge with nectarines that have been browned in a pan with a little butter and sugar.

BANANA MAPLE PORRIDGE WITH BUTTERED APPLES

It's worth buying pure maple syrup to pour over this porridge. Big bulbous Bramley apples are delicious when buttered, so are your everyday Jonathans or Granny Smiths.

1 cup rolled oats

1½ cups (12 fl oz) boiling water

1 cup (8 fl oz) milk

a pinch of salt

1 tablespoon brown sugar

2 tablespoons maple syrup

1 banana, finely sliced

to serve

buttered apples (below)

2 tablespoons maple syrup

warm milk

Place oats and boiling water in a medium saucepan and stir to combine. Let oats sit for 10 minutes. Add the remaining ingredients to oats in the saucepan and stir again. Bring slowly to the boil over medium heat. Reduce the heat, to bring the mixture to simmer. Cook for 10 minutes, stirring often. The banana should almost dissolve. Remove from heat and let the porridge stand, covered, for 2–3 minutes before serving.

to serve spoon porridge into two bowls, top with buttered apples and extra maple syrup, and offer a jug of warm milk on the side. Serves 2.

BUTTERED APPLES

30 g (1 oz) unsalted butter

½ kg (1 lb) hard sweet apples, peeled, cored and thinly sliced

1 tablespoon caster (superfine) sugar

Place butter in a frying pan and melt over medium heat. Add the apples and sprinkle with sugar. Cook gently until the undersides of the apples are pale golden. Turn the slices over very gently, to avoid breaking them, and cook until golden and translucent. Serve warm.

POACHED EGGS WITH WILTED BABY SPINACH

A low-fat alternative to our rich and creamy scrambled eggs. (Of course, you can render it just as decadent with a hollandaise sauce.) I like the spinach cooked with a little garlic.

per person
2 eggs, the fresher the better
10 g (1/4 oz) butter
200 g (6½ oz) baby spinach
1 teaspoon lemon juice
1 clove garlic, crushed (optional)
salt and freshly ground black pepper

to serve
2 thick slices of toast

In a shallow frying pan, bring 5 cm (2 in) of water to the boil. Turn off the heat and add the eggs at once. To minimise the spreading of the whites, break the eggs directly into the water, carefully opening the two halves of the shells at the water surface so that the eggs slide into the water. Cover the pan with a tight-fitting lid. Leave the eggs to cook undisturbed in the water for about 3 minutes. The eggs are cooked when the whites are opaque.

Remove the eggs from the pan with a slotted spoon and drain on a clean tea towel. Using a small knife, trim away the thin outer layer of egg white around the edge.

Melt butter in a saucepan over medium heat. Add the baby spinach, lemon juice, garlic, salt and pepper. Toss quickly until baby spinach is just wilted.

to serve Place toast on a plate, top with spinach and poached eggs.

FRENCH TOAST STUFFED WITH PEACHES

There's a time in summer when peaches are the best fruit – present them juicy and warmed in pan-fried eggy parcels. With or without a glass of champagne, it's enough to make urban sophisticates lose their reserve.

1 kg (2 lb) ripe peaches
2 tablespoons lemon juice
1/2 cup caster (superfine) sugar
4 eggs
1 cup (8 fl oz) milk
1/3 cup (2 3/4 fl oz) cream
2 teaspoons vanilla essence
1 teaspoon ground cinnamon
a pinch of nutmeg

8 slices brioche loaf, 4 cm (1 1/2 in) thick
4 tablespoons unsalted butter
to serve
maple syrup
vanilla yoghurt (below)

For a savoury breakfast, stuff the French toast with ham instead of peaches, and serve with tomato relish.

Place peaches in a large saucepan of boiling water and blanch for 10 seconds. Remove peaches with a slotted spoon and place in a bowl of iced water. When cooled, remove, peel and slice the peaches in half. Remove the stones and cut the peaches into 1 cm (1/2 in) thick slices. Toss the peach slices in a bowl with the lemon juice and 1/4 cup of the sugar and leave for 30 minutes.

Place eggs, milk, cream, vanilla, remaining sugar, cinnamon and nutmeg in a large bowl and whisk to combine.

With a sharp, thin-bladed knife, carefully slit open one side of each slice of bread to form a pocket, leaving at least 1 cm (1/2 in) around the edges. Stuff the bread pockets with 5 or 6 peach slices each. When all the bread is stuffed, pour the excess peach juice into the egg mixture. Reserve leftover peach slices for serving.

Soak the stuffed bread for 1 minute in the egg mixture, turning the slices at least once so they will be evenly moistened.

Preheat the oven to 180°C (350°F). Heat the butter in a large frying pan over medium heat. When the butter is sizzling, remove the slices from the egg mixture and place in the pan. Cook on one side until golden brown. Turn and cook until the other side is golden brown. Repeat with remaining slices. Arrange slices on a baking tray, place in the preheated oven and bake for 12 minutes, or until cooked.

Remove the toast from the oven. Serve immediately on warm plates with the reserved peach slices, maple syrup and vanilla yoghurt. Serves 4.

VANILLA YOGHURT

1 cup natural yoghurt
1 teaspoon vanilla extract
Place ingredients in small bowl and stir until combined. Refrigerate until required.

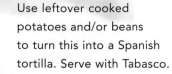

Use leftover cooked potatoes and/or beans to turn this into a Spanish tortilla. Serve with Tabasco.

OPEN-FACED OMELETTE WITH FRESH TOMATO, EMMENTHAL AND ROCKET

This simplified version of a classic folded omelette is more like an Italian frittata. Just one of many alternative combinations would be to substitute roasted peppers and fontina for the tomato and Emmenthal.

per person
3 eggs
a pinch of salt
10 g (1/4 oz) butter
2 spring onions, chopped
1 ripe tomato, sliced
2 slices of Emmenthal
1 handful rocket (arugula), tossed in a little olive oil and sea salt
black pepper

Place eggs and salt in a bowl with 2 tablespoons of water and beat lightly with a fork until just combined.

Melt butter in a small frying pan over medium heat and pour in egg mixture. As the eggs begin to cook, place chopped spring onions on top, followed by sliced tomato and Emmenthal. Continue to cook for 2–3 minutes.

Place the pan under a preheated grill to finish cooking the eggs and melt the Emmenthal. Slide the finished omelette onto a warm serving plate and place the rocket in the centre of the omelette. Finish with a grinding of black pepper.

ICED CINNAMON SNAIL ROLLS

Create your own cakeshop fragrance with this traditional recipe. Prepare Sunday snails on Saturday night, to the stage where you've rolled up the dough into a log, and refrigerate. In the morning, after slicing, the rolls will just take a little longer than usual to rise.

dough	1/3 cup currants
2 x 7 g (1/4 oz) sachets dried yeast	1/3 cup sultanas
1/4 cup (2 fl oz) lukewarm water	80 g (2 1/2 oz) unsalted butter, melted
1 cup (8 fl oz) milk	3/4 cup firmly packed brown sugar
125 g (4 oz) unsalted butter, cubed	1 tablespoon ground cinnamon
4 cups plain (all-purpose) flour	*icing*
a pinch of salt	1 cup icing (confectioners') sugar
1/4 cup (2 oz) sugar	1 tablespoon warm water
2 eggs, lightly beaten	1/2 teaspoon vanilla essence

To make the dough, dissolve the yeast in the warm water, in a small bowl. Place milk and cubed butter in a medium saucepan and heat until butter is melted. Sift flour and salt into a large mixing bowl. Add sugar and stir to combine. Make a well in the centre and add eggs, and milk and yeast mixtures. Stir until a dough forms.

Turn the dough out onto a lightly floured surface and knead for 6–8 minutes, working in extra flour if dough is too sticky. Add the currants and sultanas during the last 2 minutes of kneading. Turn the dough into a large, lightly greased bowl and cover loosely with plastic wrap. Keep the bowl in a warm place and let the dough rise for 30 minutes to an hour, or until the dough has doubled in size.

Punch the dough down and turn out onto a lightly floured bench. Roll it into a 23 x 60 cm (9 x 24 in) rectangle. Brush generously with the melted butter, reserving some for later, and sprinkle brown sugar and cinnamon evenly over the surface.

Roll the dough up from the short end, swiss-roll style, to make a log. Cut the roll, seam-side-down, into 2 cm (3/4 in) thick slices and place on baking trays that have been lightly greased, leaving 1.5 cm (5/8 in) between each slice. Brush the tops of the rolls with the remaining butter. Cover loosely and leave to rise until doubled.

Preheat oven to 180°C (350°F). Bake rolls for 20–30 minutes. Remove from the oven, allow to cool on a rack for 10 minutes, and drizzle with icing.

To make icing, place icing sugar, warm water and vanilla in a mixing bowl and stir until smooth. Add extra water if the icing is too thick to drizzle. Makes 12.

Any stone fruit benefits from the vanilla-poaching treatment. It's a useful way to use up an excess of summer produce. Serve over cereal, or with a dollop of yoghurt.

VANILLA-POACHED APRICOTS

In winter, omit the sugar and use dried apricots instead – they make a delicious syrup on their own. Try substituting cardamom pods for vanilla – they impart a spicier flavour.

200 g (6¹/2 oz) sugar
1 vanilla bean, split in half lengthways
1 kg (2 lb) ripe apricots, halved and stoned

Place sugar and vanilla bean in a large saucepan with 2 cups (16 fl oz) water and stir gently over low heat until sugar dissolves. When sugar has dissolved, stop stirring and increase heat. Boil syrup rapidly for 1 minute. Add the fruit and simmer for 10 minutes, or until the fruit is tender.

Pour the fruit and syrup into a serving dish and serve hot or cold. (These apricots will keep for up to 4 days in the refrigerator.) Serves 4.

POTATO AND FETA PANCAKES

Greece is the word... and Sydney bears some coastal relation. These rounds beat hash browns for flavour. Cook them up in a smaller size for cocktail hour.

1/2 kg (1 lb) potatoes	*to serve*
1 small onion	parsley
2 eggs	mint
2 tablespoons chopped mint	lemon wedges
1/4 cup crumbled feta cheese	
1/4 cup plain (all-purpose) flour	
salt and freshly ground black pepper	
4 tablespoons vegetable oil	

Peel and grate the potatoes and onion, stir in a little salt, and place in a colander to drain for 15–20 minutes. Place the eggs in a bowl and beat lightly. Squeeze excess moisture from the potato mix and combine with the eggs, mint, feta, flour and salt and pepper.

Heat the oil in a large non-stick frying pan. Add 2 tablespoons of mixture per pancake to the pan and squash to make flat 7 cm (2³/4 in) pancakes. Cook on both sides until golden brown. Serve garnished with fresh parsley and mint and a wedge of lemon. Makes 8–10 pancakes.

To give yoghurt
a vanilla flavour, stir
1 teaspoon of vanilla
extract into each cup
of yoghurt.

HONEYED YOGHURT WITH FRESH BERRIES

This is more a reminder than a recipe: a reminder from the Mediterranean that thick creamy
yoghurt goes well with honey, goes well with any luscious fruit.

1 1/2 cups (12 fl oz) continental-style yoghurt
3 tablespoons honey
1 cup mixed berries

Place yoghurt and 2 tablespoons of honey in bowl and mix well. Spoon into glasses
or bowls then top with the berries. Drizzle over remaining honey. Serves 2.

TOASTED GRAIN AND NUT CEREAL

You've always wished muesli had more dried figs? Choc chips? Add as many as you like of your own eccentric ingredients to this basic recipe – or sprinkle it plain over yoghurt, cut fruit, stewed rhubarb...

125 g (4 oz) unsalted butter
3/4 cup (6 fl oz) honey
1½ teaspoons vanilla essence
500 g (1 lb) rolled oats
1 cup unsalted sunflower seeds
1 cup slivered almonds
1 cup shredded coconut
3/4 cup unsalted pumpkin seeds
1 cup rye flakes
1 cup chopped dried fruit, such as sultanas, apricots or apples (optional)

Preheat oven to 170°C (325°F). Place butter, honey and vanilla in a small saucepan. Cook gently over a low heat, stirring occasionally, for 5 minutes, or until honey and butter are combined. Place remaining ingredients, except the fruit, in a large mixing bowl and mix well. Slowly stir in the butter mixture, making sure that each grain is evenly coated. Spread the cereal over a large baking dish and bake in the oven for 25 minutes, or until the grains are crisp and very lightly browned. Stir occasionally to prevent the mixture from sticking to the baking dish.

Remove cereal from the oven and allow to cool. If using dried fruit, add it at this stage and stir evenly through the grain mixture.

This muesli can be stored at room temperature in an airtight container for up to 1 month. Makes 1.5 kg (3 lb).

In many recipes strawberries are macerated in sugar, which tends to turn them a mushy brown. Using honey instead intensifies their red ripeness.

LEMON SOUFFLÉ CAKES

Feather-light and low in fat, these citrus-flavoured pancakes are the brunch choice for summer days when your skin is salt-licked and a little feverish. Pile them with fruit in season and sweeten with sugar syrup or a dusting of icing sugar.

3/4 cup (6 fl oz) buttermilk

2 egg yolks

2 tablespoons lemon juice

3 teaspoons grated lemon zest

1 teaspoon vanilla essence

25 g (3/4 oz) unsalted butter, melted

3/4 cup plain (all-purpose) flour

1 teaspoon baking powder

3 tablespoons caster (superfine) sugar

a pinch of salt

2 egg whites

to serve

200 g (6 1/2 oz) strawberries, halved

1 tablespoon honey

icing (confectioners') sugar

Place buttermilk, egg yolks, lemon juice and zest, and vanilla essence in a bowl and stir until combined. Add the melted butter and mix well.

Sift flour, baking powder, caster sugar and salt into a large bowl. Make a well in the centre and gradually stir in the buttermilk mixture until the dry ingredients are just moistened, being careful not to overmix.

Place the egg whites in a dry, clean bowl and beat until soft peaks form. Gently fold the egg whites into the batter, using a large metal spoon.

Melt a small portion of butter in a non-stick frying pan over medium heat and drop 2 tablespoons of batter per cake into the pan. Cook the cake until golden brown on the underside and looking dry at the edges, then turn and cook the other side. Transfer to a plate and keep warm while cooking remaining batter.

Toss the fresh strawberries with honey and a light dusting of icing sugar. Dust lemon soufflé cakes with icing sugar before serving with the strawberries. Serves 4.

CRUMPETS WITH BLACKBERRY BUTTER

The difference between store-bought and home-made crumpets has to be experienced at least once. You'll need electric beaters to combine the batter and special rings to shape the crumpets in the pan.

1½ cups (12 fl oz) milk
1½ teaspoons sugar
7 g (¼ oz) sachet dried yeast
375 g (12 oz) plain (all-purpose) flour
a pinch of salt

½ teaspoon bicarbonate of soda
 (baking soda)

to serve
blackberry butter (below)

Pour the milk into a saucepan and heat until just warm. Remove from heat, transfer to a bowl and stir in the sugar and yeast. (Do not have the milk too hot or it will kill the yeast.) Allow to stand for 10 minutes or until the milk starts to bubble.

Sift the flour and salt into a bowl and make a well in the centre. Gradually add the milk to the flour and beat with electric beaters until completely smooth. Cover with plastic wrap and stand in a warm place for 1–1½ hours, or until doubled in volume and full of air bubbles.

Mix the bircarbonate of soda with 200 ml (6½ fl oz) water, and use electric beaters to combine with the batter. Heat a heavy-based frying pan over medium heat and brush with melted butter. Lightly grease 4 metal rings, 8 cm (3 in) in diameter and 3 cm (1¼ in) deep, and put in the pan. Spoon approximately 3 tablespoons of the batter into each ring. Cook over a very low heat for 5 minutes or until the surface is full of large bubbles and a skin has formed. Loosen the rings and turn over to cook the other side. Remove the crumpets from the pan and stand on a wire rack covered with a tea towel while cooking the remaining batter. Serve the crumpets fresh or toasted, spread with lashings of blackberry butter. Makes about 16.

BLACKBERRY BUTTER

1 cup blackberries
1½ tablespoons sugar
1 tablespoon lemon juice
½ cup unsalted butter, softened

Place berries, sugar and lemon juice in a saucepan over high heat and bring to the boil. Reduce heat and simmer for 5 minutes or until syrupy. Remove from heat and cool completely. Place butter in a bowl and whip with a wooden spoon until light. Fold through the blackberries to create a ripple effect. Spoon into one or more ramekins, cover and refrigerate until required.

When people found out I was doing a book, many of them said they couldn't wait to discover the secret of our scrambled eggs. It might be better left an angst-free secret, but here it is – free-range eggs, a good non-stick pan, and lots of cream!

SCRAMBLED EGGS

This dish was placed first on a list of definitive Sydney flavours by the *Sydney Morning Herald*'s 'Good Living' section.

per person
2 eggs
1/3 cup (2 3/4 fl oz) cream
a pinch of salt
10 g (1/4 oz) butter

Place eggs, cream and salt in a bowl and whisk together.

Melt butter in a non-stick frying pan over high heat, taking care not to burn the butter. Pour in egg mixture and cook for 20 seconds, or until gently set around the edge. Stir the eggs with a wooden spoon, gently bringing the egg mixture on the outside of the pan to the centre. The idea is to fold the eggs rather than to scramble them. Leave to cook for 20 seconds longer and repeat the folding process. When the eggs are just set (remembering that they will continue cooking as they rest), turn out onto a plate and serve with hot toast.

note If you are making more than two serves of scrambled eggs, make sure you cook separate batches so as not to crowd the frying pan.

TOASTED COCONUT WAFFLES WITH FRESH MANGO AND PALM SYRUP

On humid Sydney mornings, when the continent seems to have drifted several degrees toward the equator, this combination completes the scene on deck. Dress code: boardshorts and sarongs.

1/2 cup shredded coconut

3 eggs, separated

50 g (11/2 oz) unsalted butter, melted

1 cup (8 fl oz) milk

1/2 cup (4 fl oz) coconut milk

1/2 teaspoon vanilla essence

1 cup plain (all-purpose) flour

a pinch of salt

2 teaspoons bicarbonate of soda
 (baking soda)

3 tablespoons caster (superfine)
 sugar

to serve

fresh mango

palm syrup (see note)

Preheat the oven to 180°C (350°F). Spread the coconut on a baking tray, place in the oven, and toast for about 10 minutes, or until golden brown. Set aside to cool.

Place egg yolks, melted butter, milk, coconut milk, vanilla and toasted coconut in a mixing bowl and stir to combine.

Sift flour, salt, bicarbonate of soda and sugar in a bowl and make a well in the centre. Gradually stir in coconut mixture until just combined.

Place egg whites in a clean dry bowl and beat until soft peaks form. Fold egg whites through the batter, using a large metal spoon.

Cook the waffles in a waffle iron according to the manufacturer's instructions.

Serve with slices of fresh mango, pour palm syrup over the mango slices and then place another waffle on top. Serves 4.

note If palm syrup is unavailable, use palm sugar to make your own: grate 100 g (31/2 oz) palm sugar into a saucepan, add 1 cup (8 fl oz) water and dissolve over medium heat. Continue cooking until the syrup is reduced by about half and allow to cool before spooning over waffles.

ROAST MUSHROOMS WITH THYME AND TALEGGIO

This variation on mushrooms on toast is juicy, more-ish... oozing with Italian meltdown.

8 large field (portobello) mushrooms
(about 10 cm/4 in diameter)
1 tablespoon roughly chopped
thyme
4 tablespoons extra virgin olive oil
juice of 1 lemon
1 large clove garlic, cut into 8 slivers
200 g (6½ oz) baby spinach, washed
150 g (5 oz) Italian Taleggio cheese, sliced

to serve
4 thick slices of toast
1 tablespoon balsamic vinegar

Preheat the oven to 200°C (400°F). Place the mushrooms in a roasting tin. Mix thyme, olive oil and lemon juice together and pour over the mushrooms. Place a slice of garlic on each mushroom and bake the mushrooms for 10 minutes in the oven.

Meanwhile, place the spinach (undried, with water clinging to the leaves) in a frying pan over medium heat and turn with a spatula until wilted.

Remove the mushrooms from the oven. Top each mushroom with a little spinach and some sliced Taleggio. Return to the oven for 5–6 minutes, until the cheese has melted. Place 2 mushrooms on each slice of toast. Drizzle with pan juices and balsamic vinegar. Serves 4.

BREAKFAST DRINKS + NIBBLES

Brunch can be the most relaxed event, with guests following the aromas of baking and fresh coffee up the driveway. Savouries on toast are easily made for any size crowd.

BLUEBERRY AND BRAN MUFFINS

30 g (1 oz) butter

3/4 cup (6 fl oz) honey

1/2 cup (4 fl oz) milk

1/2 cup (4 fl oz) vegetable oil

3 eggs

3 cups plain (all-purpose) flour

2 teaspoons baking powder

1/2 cup bran cereal

1 1/2 teaspoons ground cinnamon

1 apple, grated

2 bananas, mashed

250 g (8 oz) blueberries

6 strawberries, halved

Preheat the oven to 180°C (350°F). Place butter and honey in a small saucepan and cook over medium heat for 5 minutes or until slightly caramelised.

Place milk, vegetable oil and eggs in a bowl and whisk.

Place flour, baking powder, bran and cinnamon in a bowl and mix to combine. Stir apple, bananas and blueberries through flour. Add milk mixture and stir until dry ingredients are just moistened. Then fold in butter mixture until just combined, being careful not to overmix.

Set out 2 six-hole muffin trays with paper liners. Spoon muffin batter into each cup. Top each muffin with a strawberry half. Bake in the oven for 25–30 minutes or until the tops are golden and a skewer comes out clean. Cool slightly, remove cups from tray and serve. Makes 12.

MANGO AND BANANA SUNRISE DRINK

1 cup (8 fl oz) orange juice

1/2 cup chopped mango

1/2 ripe banana

2 tablespoons yoghurt

Place all ingredients in a blender. Blend until smooth. Serves 1–2.

AVOCADO TOAST WITH LIME, PEPPER AND CORIANDER

2 tablespoons lime juice
2 tablespoons olive oil
sea salt
freshly ground pepper
1 avocado, peeled and quartered
4 slices sourdough bread, toasted
coriander (cilantro) leaves

Place lime juice, olive oil, salt and pepper in a bowl and whisk until combined.

Serve quarters of avocado on toast, drizzled with dressing and topped with coriander, sea salt and lots of freshly ground pepper. Serves 4.

SPICY VIRGIN MARY

2 cups (16 fl oz) tomato juice
juice of 1 lime
8 drops Tabasco
sea salt
freshly cracked black pepper
ice

to serve
sea salt
2 lime quarters

Chill 2 glasses for 1 hour in a refrigerator.

Place tomato and lime juice, Tabasco, salt and pepper in a cocktail shaker with a handful of ice. Shake all ingredients until combined.

Place a layer of sea salt in a saucer and rub a quarter of lime around the rim of 2 glasses. Dip the rim of the glasses into salt. Strain Virgin Marys into the glasses, being careful not to disturb the salt rim. Serve with lime wedges. Serves 2.

LUNCH

Around noon,
Nielsen Park, Vaucluse

LUNCH REVIVES THE SENSES

SYDNEY HITS THE PAVEMENT AND FOLLOWS ITS NOSE. THERE'S TEXTURE IN LENTIL SOUP BROUGHT FROM HOME; A LEFTOVER SLICE OF THE WEEKEND'S RICOTTA AND TOMATO TART NEEDS NOTHING EXTRA IF SAVOURED ON A BENCH WITH A VIEW OF CIRCULAR QUAY; OR PLUNGE INTO CHINATOWN FOR AN HOUR'S ESCAPE FROM THE WEST, SUBMERGING THE TASTE-BUDS IN BROTH WITH NOODLES AND WOK-CRISPED VEGETABLES. MORE LEISURELY LUNCHES FOLLOW SATURDAY SHOPPING AND DOMESTIC FLURRIES. THEY MARK THE REAL BEGINNING OF TIME OFF. THE RUSTLE OF NEWSPAPERS SETTLES INTO THE POSSIBILITY OF BAKING A CAKE, WEIGHING UP MOVIE REVIEWS, SNOOZING TO THE SOUND OF CRICKET ON THE TELEVISION.

CORN AND GINGER SOUP

This is fast food. It takes next to no time to make, and you'll want to lick the bowl.

1 tablespoon vegetable oil
½ cup finely sliced spring (green)
  onions
1 tablespoon finely sliced ginger
2 cups corn kernels, cut from cobs
1 litre (24 fl oz) chicken stock or water
1 tablespoon shao hsing wine
¼ teaspoon white pepper
1 teaspoon sugar
1 teaspoon salt

2 tablespoons soy sauce
to serve
2 tablespoons sliced spring onions
coriander (cilantro) sprigs
1 teaspoon sesame oil

Heat oil in a large saucepan over medium heat. Add spring onions and ginger and stir-fry for 1 minute. Add corn and continue stirring for another minute. Pour in stock, or water, and bring to the boil. Season with wine, pepper, sugar, salt and soy sauce. Simmer for a further 5 minutes.

to serve Ladle into bowls and sprinkle with spring onion and coriander, and drizzle with a few drops of sesame oil. Serves 6–8.

If pressed for time, serve with a simple dressing made from extra virgin olive oil and the juice of fresh limes.

SUMMER POACHED CHICKEN SALAD

This is the kind of clean, uncomplicated dish you start to long for when you're sitting at your desk and the GPO clock finishes its midday gong. Luckily, it packs well, with the dressing on the side.

3 coriander (cilantro) roots with stems
1 tablespoon black peppercorns
3 slices fresh ginger
2 spring (green) onions, roughly chopped
1 tablespoon salt
4 chicken breast fillets
to serve
1/2 iceberg lettuce, shredded
2 cups baby english spinach

1 cup broccoli florets, blanched and refreshed
1 cup sugarsnap peas, blanched and refreshed
8 asparagus spears, blanched and refreshed
chilli garlic dressing (below)
1/2 cup coriander (cilantro) leaves
1/4 cup mint leaves
lime wedges

Place coriander roots, peppercorns, ginger, onions and salt in a medium to large saucepan, fill with cold water and bring to the boil over high heat. Add chicken breasts to saucepan and stir. Turn off heat and cover with a tight-fitting lid. Leave to poach for 2 hours.

to serve Divide iceberg lettuce, spinach and blanched vegetables among four plates. Slice chicken breasts on the diagonal into 1 cm (1/2 in) slices. Place on top of greens and spoon over dressing. Finish with coriander, mint leaves and lime wedges. Serves 4.

CHILLI GARLIC DRESSING

2 chillies, finely chopped
3 cloves garlic, chopped
2 tablespoons palm sugar

1 tablespoon rice vinegar
3 tablespoons lime or lemon juice
3 tablespoons fish sauce

Place all ingredients in a bowl and whisk to combine.

PUY LENTIL SOUP WITH PARMESAN TOASTS

Puy lentils cook quickly, and hold their texture during the cooking process, where larger lentils tend to turn to dhal. Make an armada of Parmesan toasts – after the first fleet you'll find they take over the cookie jar.

50 g (1 1/2 oz) butter	1 litre (32 fl oz) vegetable stock, or
1 tablespoon olive oil	water
1/2 cup chopped carrots	2 bay leaves
1/2 cup chopped spanish onion	2 tablespoons chopped fresh oregano
1/2 cup sliced leek, white part only	1/2 cup lentils du Puy
1/2 cup chopped celery	1 teaspoon salt
4 cloves garlic, finely chopped	freshly ground black pepper
1 small red chilli, finely chopped	1/2 cup finely chopped parsley
400 g (13 oz) tin chopped Italian	*to serve*
tomatoes	Parmesan toasts (below)

Melt butter and oil in a large saucepan over medium heat. Add carrots, onion and leeks and cook for 10 minutes, stirring occasionally. Add celery, garlic and chilli and cook for a further 5 minutes. Add chopped tomatoes, stock (or water), bay leaves, oregano and lentils and bring to the boil. Reduce heat and simmer, stirring occasionally, for 30 minutes. Season with salt and pepper, and stir through parsley.

Ladle into serving bowls and serve with Parmesan toasts. Serves 4.

PARMESAN TOASTS

1/4 cup (2 fl oz) extra virgin olive oil	freshly ground black pepper
2 cloves garlic	3/4 cup finely grated Parmigiano
1/2 baguette	Reggiano cheese
sea salt	

Preheat the oven to 200°C (400°F).

Place oil and garlic in a blender and process until smooth.

Slice the baguette into thin slices. Lay the slices in one layer on a baking tray. Using a pastry brush, brush each piece of baguette with the garlic oil. Sprinkle generously with salt and pepper and top with Parmesan cheese. Bake the toasts for 15–20 minutes, or until they are brown and crisp. Serve at room temperature. Makes 20 pieces.

note Toast will keep in an airtight container for up to 1 week.

To make lemon butter, heat the juice
of two lemons in a small pan over
medium heat; whisk in 125 g (4 oz)
unsalted butter in small pieces until
melted and combined. Season with
salt and freshly ground black pepper.

SPRING ONION PANCAKE WITH GRAVLAX

This variation on blinis has been on bills menu for years and is a favourite with Sydney's ladies
who lunch. To serve as canapés, make the pancakes slightly larger, spread the topping
evenly, roll up and slice, securing each spiral with a toothpick.

2 eggs
1 cup (8 fl oz) milk
40 g (1¼ oz) butter, melted, cooled
125 g (4 oz) plain (all-purpose) flour
2½ teaspoons baking powder
½ teaspoon salt
50 g (1½ oz) spring (green) onions,
  sliced

to serve
4 cups baby english spinach
16 slices gravlax
1 telegraph cucumber,
  cut into ribbons with a
  vegetable peeler
125 g (4 oz) lemon butter (see above)

Place eggs, milk and melted butter in a bowl and whisk until combined. Sift flour,
baking powder and salt into a bowl. Make a well in the centre, gradually add egg
mixture and beat until smooth. Allow to rest for 2 hours (or overnight, if possible).

Heat a non-stick frying pan and ladle 4 tablespoons of batter into the pan.
Sprinkle 1 tablespoon of spring onions over pancake. Cook for around 2 minutes
until bubbles appear on the surface of pancake. Turn pancake and cook on the
other side. Transfer to a plate and keep warm while cooking remaining pancakes.

to serve Place a pancake on each plate, top with 1 cup of baby spinach, 4 slices
of gravlax and a pile of cucumber ribbons. Spoon lemon butter around, but not on
top of, the pancake. Serves 4.

SPAGHETTINI WITH CRAB, LIME AND CHILLI

An Asian-European fusion recipe that really works – perhaps because spaghettini is closely related to the egg noodle. This dish relies on the hot pasta to warm the other ingredients, so combine immediately after draining.

150 g (5 oz) crab meat
juice and zest of 2 limes
juice of 1 lemon
1 clove garlic, crushed
1/4 cup chopped parsley
1/4 cup chopped spring (green) onions
1 small red chilli, finely chopped
1 teaspoon sea salt
freshly ground black pepper
1/4 cup (2 fl oz) extra virgin olive oil
200 g (61/2 oz) spaghettini

Place crab, lime and lemon juices, lime zest, garlic, parsley, spring onions, chilli, sea salt and pepper in a bowl and stir in olive oil to combine. Taste to adjust the seasoning.

Cook spaghettini in rapidly boiling salted water in a large saucepan, according to manufacturer's instructions. Drain well.

Toss pasta into crab mixture and serve in individual bowls. Serves 2.

GOATS CURD AND LENTIL SALAD WITH ROASTED BEETROOT

In recent years the collective Australian herd of goats has grown to provide us with a wide variety of products, from tangy and fresh, to pungent and mature. Curd is much lighter on the palate than cheese, which makes it a perfect salad ingredient.

4 medium-sized beetroot	1 tablespoon finely chopped mint
2 tablespoons olive oil	1/4 cup finely chopped parsley
sea salt	*to serve*
freshly ground black pepper	mint leaves
I cup lentils du Puy	8 asparagus spears,
1/4 cup diced red onion	blanched and cooled
1/4 cup seeded and diced tomato	mint leaves
3 tablespoons extra virgin olive oil	200 g (61/2 oz) goats curd
1 tablespoon balsamic vinegar	extra virgin olive oil to drizzle

Preheat oven to 220°C (440°F). Place beetroot in a small baking dish and drizzle with the olive oil, salt and pepper. Cover with foil and place in the oven for 40–45 minutes, or until beetroots are tender when pierced wtih a knife. Remove from oven and allow to cool. Set aside.

Place lentils with 1 1/2 cups (12 fl oz) of water in a medium saucepan and bring to the boil. Reduce heat and simmer for 15 minutes. Strain.

Place warm lentils, red onion, tomato, extra virgin olive oil, vinegar, salt and pepper in a bowl, stir and set aside.

Peel beetroots by rubbing the skins gently with your hands until they come off. Slice beetroot vertically into 1 cm (1/2 in) slices.

Stir mint and parsley through lentils.

to serve Divide lentils among four plates, top with a few sprigs of mint and the asparagus. Using a large spoon dipped in hot water, top with spoonfuls of goats curd. Finish with slices of beetroot and drizzle with extra virgin olive oil. Serves 4.

FINE STEAK SANDWICH WITH GARLIC CRÈME

On the menu at bills from the start, this dish is probably a success because it delivers an Australian favourite from the days of the corner milkbar, in a slightly more sophisticated form. Use a bread that will soak up the steak juices.

3 tablespoons olive oil
1 cup finely sliced onion
2 tablespoons balsamic vinegar
sea salt
freshly ground black pepper
4 thin slices sirlion or fillet steak
8 thick slices bread, such as ciabatta
garlic crème (below)
1 bunch rocket (arugula), washed and dried
4 ripe tomatoes, sliced

Heat 2 tablespoons of the olive oil in a large frying pan over medium heat, add the onion and cook for 10 minutes, stirring frequently, until golden. Add vinegar, salt and pepper and cook for a minute longer until caramelised. Remove onion from the pan and set aside.

Using the same pan, heat the remaining olive oil over high heat. Add steak to the pan and sprinkle with salt and pepper. Cook for 1 minute, turn and cook the other side for a further minute.

Spread the bread with garlic crème. Place rocket on 4 of the slices and top with tomatoes. Place onions on top of tomato, followed by steak. Top with a second slice of bread. Serves 4.

GARLIC CRÈME

2 egg yolks
1 tablespoon balsamic vinegar
2 cloves garlic, crushed

sea salt
freshly ground black pepper
1 cup (8 fl oz) canola, or other mild oil

Place egg yolks, vinegar, garlic, salt and pepper in a bowl (or in a food processor) and whisk until combined. Add the oil drop by drop, whisking constantly. When the sauce starts to thicken, add the oil in a steady stream until the oil is fully incorporated. If the crème is too thick, thin with a tablespoon of warm water.

CHICKEN NOODLE SOUP WITH LEMON

Vietnamese pho meets Jewish chicken soup in a clear broth with fresh things thrown in. Rather than assembling everything in the bowls, you can put dishes of herbs, beansprouts and lemon slices on the table for guests to add themselves.

6 cups (48 fl oz) chicken stock (below)
1½ cups shredded chicken (below)
9 ears baby corn, sliced in
   half lengthways
1½ cups chopped green vegetables,
   such as bok choy
3 sheets (10 x 15 cm) (4 x 6 in) fresh
   lasagne, torn into 5 cm (2 in) squares
3 teaspoons lemon juice

3 teaspoons fish sauce
1½ red chillies, sliced (optional)
12 mint leaves
3/4 cup coriander (cilantro) leaves
thin slices of lemon

Prepare chicken stock and chicken (see below). Place chicken stock in a saucepan over high heat. Add chicken, corn and green vegetables and cook for about 1 minute, until vegetables are just tender.

Cook the lasagne pieces in salted boiling water (stirring occasionally, to keep them from sticking together) until tender. Drain.

Place lasagne, lemon juice, fish sauce and chilli in a large soup bowl and pour soup over the top. Finish with mint and coriander leaves and slices of lemon. Serves 6–8.

CHICKEN STOCK

1 x 1.5 kg (3 lb) chicken
4 slices fresh ginger
2 spring (green) onions, cut into 10 cm (4 in) lengths
1 teaspoon black peppercorns

Rinse chicken inside and out. Pat dry. Put chicken, ginger, spring onions and peppercorns in a large saucepan with 4 litres of cold water. Bring to a near boil over high heat and reduce the heat to maintain a steady simmer. After 5–10 minutes, use a large shallow spoon to skim off and discard scum.

Simmer the stock undisturbed for 3 hours. Strain stock and shred chicken.

RICOTTA AND TOMATO TART

It travels well and tastes best at room temperature. All you need is a salad, wine and fresh fruit to make a meal of it, at the Harbour's edge, or in one of Sydney's many parks, in the shade of a Moreton Bay fig tree.

2 ripe tomatoes, finely sliced
sea salt
1 quantity rough puff pastry (below)
2 cups ricotta
2 eggs, lightly beaten
1/4 cup cream
1/4 cup finely grated Parmesan
a pinch of ground nutmeg
freshly ground black pepper

1 cup finely shredded rocket (arugula)
1 egg yolk, lightly beaten, for glazing
2 tablespoons finely chopped parsley

Preheat the oven to 200°C (400°F). Place tomatoes in a colander, sprinkle with salt and leave to drain. Place pastry dough on a lightly floured surface and roll out to a circle about 35 cm (14 in) in diameter and 3 mm (1/4 in) thick. Place the dough on a lightly floured baking tray.

Place ricotta, eggs, cream, Parmesan, nutmeg, salt and pepper in a bowl and mix well. Add rocket and stir to combine. Place this ricotta mixture in the centre of the dough, and spread the filling over the dough, leaving a 5 cm (2 in) border around the outside. Using your hand, lift and push the border onto the filling. Arrange tomato slices over the top of the filling. Brush pastry with egg yolks and bake in the oven for 35–40 minutes or until golden. Serve sprinkled with chopped parsley and freshly ground black pepper. Serves 8.

ROUGH PUFF PASTRY

200 g (6½ oz) plain (all-purpose) flour
1/2 teaspoon salt
200 g (6½ oz) chilled unsalted butter, cut into small pieces
2 tablespoons chilled water

Place flour and salt in a bowl, add butter and rub through with fingertips until the mixture resembles large breadcrumbs. Add enough cold water, cutting in with a knife, to form a ball. Wrap the dough in plastic wrap and refrigerate for 30 minutes.

Roll out dough into a 30 x 15 cm (12 x 6 in) rectangle. Fold in the two short ends to meet in the centre, then fold in again. Roll the pastry into a 30 x 15 cm (12 x 6 in) rectangle again, and repeat folding process. Refrigerate as a small rectangle for a further 30 minutes before using.

Chive oil adds a sophisticated finish to this and other dishes. Combine half a bunch of chopped chives and a cup of canola oil in the blender. It keeps for a week in the fridge.

TUNA SALAD WITH SOY-MIRIN DRESSING

Inspired by Nobu in New York, this dish could also be described as a cross dressing between carpaccio and sushi. The soy mirin mix is delicious over cold soba noodles tossed with slivered snowpeas and toasted sesame seeds.

2 tablespoons black peppercorns, ground
1 tablespoon sea salt
1/4 cup finely chopped coriander
1/4 cup finely chopped parsley
1/4 cup (2 fl oz) olive oil
500 g (1 lb) tuna, cut into large batons, roughly 5 cm (2 in) square at ends

to serve
1 cup shredded daikon (white radish)
1 cup shredded cucumber
1/4 cup mint leaves
1/4 cup coriander (cilantro) leaves
1/2 cup (4 fl oz) soy-mirin dressing (below)
chive oil (optional)

Place pepper, salt, coriander, parsley and olive oil in a bowl and stir to combine. Place tuna on a plate and pour over the herb mixture, pressing it on all sides of the tuna batons with your hands. Heat a large non-stick frying pan over high heat, add tuna and cook for 20 seconds on each side of the batons. Remove from pan and allow to rest for up to 1 hour.

to serve Slice tuna finely in 5 mm slices and arrange on individual plates. Top with daikon and cucumber, and mint and coriander leaves. Pour 3 tablespoons of dressing over each serve, and drizzle with chive oil (optional). Serves 4.

SOY-MIRIN DRESSING

1/2 cup (4 fl oz) mirin
1/2 cup (4 fl oz) soy sauce
3 tablespoons seasoned rice wine vinegar
Place mirin, soy sauce and vinegar in a bowl and stir. Refrigerate until required.

INDIVIDUAL CHICKEN AND LEEK PIES

An under-utilised winter vegetable, the leek releases a warm, piquant onion-like flavour when cooked that really gets behind chicken. And who can resist an individual pie?

1/2 cup plain (all-purpose) flour
1/2 teaspoon cayenne pepper
1/2 teaspoon white pepper
1 teaspoon salt
500 g (1 lb) chicken breast fillets, cut into
   2 cm (1/2 in) dice
2 tablespoons olive oil
25 g (3/4 oz) butter
2 leeks, white part only, sliced
2 cloves garlic, crushed
1/3 cup (23/4 fl oz) white wine, or water
1 cup (8 fl oz) chicken stock, or water
1/2 cup (4 fl oz) cream
1 cup fresh peas, boiled for 5 minutes
1 tablespoon chopped tarragon
1/4 cup chopped parsley
300 g (10 oz) ready-made puff pastry, in a block or 4 sheets
2 egg yolks, lighly beaten
egg yolk for glazing

I serve these pies with a green salad tossed with lots of herbs, such as chervil and parsley; or with a potato and celeriac purée in winter.

Place flour, peppers and salt in a bowl and stir. Add chicken and toss well. Shake off any excess flour. Heat oil and butter in a frying pan over high heat. Add chicken pieces and stir-fry until lightly browned and sealed, but not cooked all the way through. Remove chicken from pan and set aside.

Place leeks and garlic in the pan and cook over medium heat for 5 minutes, or until soft and wilted. Add wine and boil for 1 minute. Add stock and cream and simmer gently for a further 5 minutes. Add chicken, peas and tarragon and cook for a minute longer. Remove from heat and let cool. Stir in parsley.

Preheat oven to 180°C (350°F). Roll out pastry on a lightly floured surface until 4 mm (1/4 in) thick. Cut pastry to line bases, sides and tops of six 91/2 cm (31/2 in) pie tins. Spoon filling in pastry cases and brush edges with egg yolk. Place tops on pies, and seal with a fork. Brush tops with egg yolk and make three piercings with a sharp knife in the top of each pie.

Bake on the bottom oven shelf for 35 minutes, or until golden brown. Serves 4.

The curry dressing is also delicious over freshly cooked baby potatoes sprinkled with chopped coriander, and served with grilled chicken.

GRILLED SCALLOPS WITH CURRIED NOODLES

Fresh, springy-fleshed scallops on the half shell are becoming more consistently available, from natural and farmed beds off Tasmania, Victoria and South Australia. At the markets, ask to sniff them – they should smell clean, resting in their own sauce-catching dish.

1 tablespoon peanut oil

2 tablespoons finely chopped garlic

2 tablespoons Indian
  Madras curry paste

1/2 teaspoon turmeric

1 teaspoon salt

1 teaspoon sugar

1 cup (8 fl oz) coconut milk

3 teaspoons lime juice

2 tablespoons soy sauce

250 g (8 oz) angel hair pasta

12 scallops in their shells

chervil leaves

vegetable oil for frying

Place peanut oil in a saucepan or wok over medium heat. Add garlic and stir-fry for 30 seconds. Add curry paste, turmeric, salt, sugar, coconut milk, lime juice and soy, and simmer for 5 minutes.

Place pasta in rapidly boiling water and cook according to manufacturer's instructions. Drain and toss with about two-thirds of the curry dressing.

Remove scallops from the shell with a sharp knife, and trim off the dark strings of intestinal tract. Rinse shells until clean, and dry with paper towel. Place 3 shells on each large plate with some chervil leaves on each shell. Place angel hair pasta in one large, warmed bowl and set aside.

Heat non-stick frying pan over high heat for 2 minutes. Add vegetable oil and heat. Add scallops and cook for 2 minutes, then turn and cook for 1 minute. Remove from pan, place 1 scallop on each shell and spoon a little curry dressing over each and serve with pasta. Serves 4.

SPRING VEGETABLE SOUP

In recent years, the quality and variety of vegetables sold by Sydney greengrocers has experienced a resurgence. Seasonality is our buzzword. This soup, light and nourishing, filled with spring vigour, reflects everything that's positive about our food supply.

25 g (3/4 oz) butter
1/2 cup sliced leeks, white part only
1/3 cup diced celery
1/3 cup unpeeled, diced red potato
1/3 cup diced turnip
3 cups (24 fl oz) vegetable stock
 (below)
sea salt
freshly ground black pepper

1/3 cup freshly shucked corn kernels
1/3 cup diced zucchini
1/3 cup chopped green beans
1/2 cup ripe peeled, chopped tomatoes
1/3 cup peas
to serve
1/3 cup parsley, chopped
Parmesan toasts (see page 76)

Melt butter in a large saucepan over medium heat. Add leek, celery, potato and turnip and cook, stirring frequently, for 5 minutes. Add vegetable stock, salt and pepper and bring to the boil. Lower heat and add remaining ingredients. Simmer gently for 5 minutes until vegetables are just tender.

Ladle into bowls and top with chopped parsley. Pass around Parmesan toasts and lots of freshly ground black pepper. Serves 2.

VEGETABLE STOCK

2 tablespoons olive oil
500 g (1 lb) onions, chopped
500 g (1 lb) carrots, chopped
250 g (8 oz) parsnips, chopped
2 celery sticks including leaves,
 chopped
6 cloves garlic, crushed
2 leeks, white part only, sliced

4 sping (green) onions, chopped
 into 6 cm (21/2 in) lengths
1 bunch parsley, roughly chopped
1 teaspoon black peppercorns
4 bay leaves
1 tablespoon salt

Heat oil in a large saucepan over medium heat. Add onion, carrot, parsnip, celery and garlic and stir-fry for 5 minutes. Add remaining ingredients and 2 litres of water, and bring to the boil. Reduce heat to a simmer and cook for 1 hour. Allow to cool, then strain. Leftover stock keeps well in the freezer. Makes 2 litres.

GRILLED CHICKEN CLUB WITH AVOCADO MAYONNAISE, ROAST TOMATO AND BACON

It's probably the one truly international dish, and always reminds me of late-night hotel suppers. A good club sandwich revives the jet-lagged, the dance-party animal, or the shopper.

2 tablespoons olive oil	avocado mayonnaise (below)
4 chicken thigh fillets	1 bunch rocket (arugula), washed, dried
sea salt	4 rashers bacon, cooked
freshly ground black pepper	12 roast tomato halves (below)
8 thick slices bread	1/2 iceberg lettuce, cut into wedges

For a twist on the traditional, try marinating the chicken in Chinese Char Sieu marinade, available from Asian food stores.

Heat oil in a frying pan over high heat. Place chicken fillets in the pan, season with salt and pepper and cook for 3 minutes. Turn, season again and cook for a further 3 minutes, or until cooked through. Remove from pan, rest and cut into 1 cm (1/2 in) slices.

To make sandwiches, spread slices of bread with avocado mayonnaise. Top 4 slices of bread with rocket, chicken, bacon and roast tomato. Finish with remaining bread slices. Serve with wedges of iceberg lettuce. Serves 4.

AVOCADO MAYONNAISE

2 egg yolks	sea salt
juice and zest of 2 lemons	freshly ground black pepper
1 avocado, chopped	200 ml (6 1/2 fl oz) canola or other mild oil

Place egg yolks, lemon juice and zest, avocado, salt and pepper in a food processor and blend until combined. Add the oil, drop by drop, blending constantly. When the sauce starts to thicken, add the oil in a stream until fully incorporated. If the mayonnaise is too thick, thin with a tablespoon of warm water.

ROAST TOMATOES

6 ripe Roma tomatoes, sliced in half lengthways
4 tablespoons extra virgin olive oil
sea salt
freshly ground black pepper

Preheat the oven to 180°C (350°F). Place tomatoes on a baking tray, cut-side-up, and drizzle with olive oil. Sprinkle liberally with sea salt and pepper. Bake in the oven for 40 minutes.

SMOKED TROUT WITH POTATO SALAD

Potato and lemon – one bland and the other citrus-zesty – are the ideal flavour complements to smoked fish.

100 ml (3½ fl oz) extra virgin olive oil
50 ml (1¾ fl oz) lemon juice
1 tablespoon red wine vinegar
1 clove garlic, crushed with
  a little sea salt
sea salt
freshly ground black pepper
2 tablespoons chopped mint
¼ cup chopped parsley
¼ cup finely sliced spring (green) onions

1 stalk celery, diced
1 tablespoon baby capers
500 g (1 lb) unpeeled waxy potatoes
  (eg kipfler, chats)
250 g (8 oz) smoked rainbow trout
  (skin and bones removed)
to serve
lemon mayonnaise (below)

Place olive oil, lemon juice, red wine vinegar, garlic, salt and pepper in a bowl and whisk until combined. Stir in herbs, spring onions, celery and capers.

Cook potatoes in a large saucepan full of salted boiling water until tender when pierced with a knife. Drain and allow to cool for 5 minutes before peeling and slicing. Add potatoes to dressing while still warm. Stir gently to combine.

Divide potato salad among four plates, top with flaked smoked trout and drizzle with lemon mayonnaise. Serves 4.

LEMON MAYONNAISE

1 egg yolk
50 ml (1¾ fl oz) lemon juice
zest of 1 lemon
sea salt
freshly ground black pepper
100 ml (3⅓ fl oz) canola or other mild oil

Place egg yolk, lemon juice and zest, salt and pepper in a bowl (or food processor) and whisk until combined. Add the oil drop by drop, whisking constantly. When the sauce starts to thicken, add the oil in a steady stream until fully incorporated. If the mayonnaise is too thick, thin with a tablespoon of warm water. Keeps in the refrigerator for 5 days.

SPICED LENTIL SALAD WITH PRAWNS AND MINT YOGHURT DRESSING

Indian spices give the flavour to this salad and the mint yoghurt dressing could be served as a lassi (a yoghurt drink) if you blend with a little water and omit the fish sauce.

If you can find it, use fresh turmeric in the prawn marinade, grating a 2 cm (1/2 in) piece of the tuber into the oil mixture.

1 cup lentils du Puy
1/4 cup finely sliced spring (green) onions
1/2 cup (4 fl oz) olive oil
2 tablespoons red wine vinegar
1 green chilli, finely chopped
sea salt
freshly ground black pepper
1 teaspoon ground coriander
1 teaspoon ground cumin

1/4 cup coriander (cilantro) leaves
1 teaspoon turmeric
20 green (raw) prawns, peeled and deveined, tails intact
to serve
1 cup baby spinach leaves
100 g (31/3 oz) green beans, blanched and refreshed
mint yoghurt dressing (below)

Place lentils and 11/2 cups (12 fl oz) of water in a medium saucepan and bring to the boil. Reduce heat and simmer for 15 minutes. Drain the lentils.

Place warm lentils, spring (green) onions, 4 tablespoons of the olive oil, vinegar, chilli, salt, pepper, ground coriander, cumin and fresh coriander in a bowl, stir to combine and set aside.

Place remaining olive oil, turmeric, salt and pepper in a bowl and stir to combine. Add prawns and stir to coat with oil.

Heat a non-stick frying pan over high heat for 2 minutes. Add prawns and cook until just opaque, shaking pan frequently.

To assemble salad, divide lentils among 4 plates, top with baby spinach leaves, green beans and prawns. Finish with a drizzle of yoghurt dressing. Serves 4.

MINT YOGHURT DRESSING

1 cup yoghurt
2 tablespoons lime juice

2 teaspoons fish sauce
4 tablespoons finely chopped mint

Place all ingredients in a bowl and whisk to combine.

SPICY CHICKEN SALAD WITH LIME

This dish takes its cue from a northern Chinese shredded chicken salad. You could use a whole chicken, poach it and reserve the stock for other recipes.

4 chicken breast fillets, skin on
olive oil
sea salt
freshly ground black pepper
1 cucumber
1 cup coriander (cilantro) sprigs
   (including stalks)
1 cup mint leaves
1 teaspoon ground Szechuan
   peppercorns

1 tablespoon fish sauce
1 teaspoon sesame oil
3 tablespoons lime juice
2 spring (green) onions, thinly sliced
   on the diagonal
to serve
2 cups finely shredded iceberg lettuce
lime wedges

Preheat oven to 200°C (400°F). Brush chicken with olive oil and sprinkle with salt and pepper. Place chicken, skin-side-down, in a preheated frying pan over high heat. Sear for 2 minutes on each side, turning only once. Transfer to a baking tray and place in the oven for 15 minutes, or until the juices run clear when the flesh is pierced with a skewer. Remove from the oven and leave to rest for 20 minutes. Shred chicken into thin strips.

Slice the cucumber in half lengthways, scoop out the seeds with a small spoon, and slice the flesh thinly on the diagonal.

Place chicken, cucumber, coriander and mint in a large bowl. Sprinkle with Szechuan pepper, fish sauce, sesame oil, lime juice and spring onions and toss until well combined.

to serve Divide iceberg lettuce among four plates, and pile chicken mixture on top. Serve with extra lime wedges. Serves 4.

A green papaya salad complements fresh grilled fish, prawns or chicken, creating the perfect low-fat dinner.

GREEN PAPAYA SALAD WITH CHARGRILLED BEEF

I learned about green papaya while holidaying on an island off the Thai coast. A mother-and-daughter team made their tiny village restaurant a destination in itself by serving a salad like this. I've simplified it a little, but it still has the island flavour.

2 cloves garlic, crushed

1 red chilli, finely chopped

1 tablespoon palm sugar

3 tablespoons lime juice

2 tablespoons fish sauce

1½ cups julienned or finely
   shredded green papaya

½ cup shredded cucumber

2 spring (green) onions, finely sliced

¼ cup Thai basil leaves

¼ cup mint leaves

¼ cup coriander (cilantro) leaves

2 sirloin steaks

peanut oil

cracked black pepper

2 x 15 cm (6 in) square pieces of
   banana leaf (optional)

lime wedges (optional)

Place garlic, chilli, palm sugar, lime juice and fish sauce in a bowl and stir to dissolve. Place papaya, cucumber, spring onion, basil, mint and coriander in a bowl. Pour in garlic mixture and toss to combine.

Brush both sides of the steaks with oil. Sprinkle with cracked pepper. Barbecue or grill over medium to high heat for 3 minutes on each side. Rest for 5 minutes before slicing.

Place one banana leaf in the centre of each plate and top with papaya salad and slices of beef. Serve with lime wedges if desired. Serves 2.

BLUEBERRY BUTTER CAKE

For an old-fashioned Sydney experience you'd use mulberries from the tree that always stained your mother's washing on a windy day – and get your fingers and lips red in the picking. The blueberry is more urbane.

topping
1 cup firmly packed brown sugar
1/4 cup plain (all-purpose) flour
75 g (21/2 oz) unsalted butter, cold
cake
2 cups plain (all-purpose) flour
2 teaspoons baking powder
1/4 teaspoon salt
125 g (4 oz) unsalted butter, softened

1 cup caster (superfine) sugar
3 eggs, lightly beaten
1 cup sour cream
2 cups blueberries

To make the topping, place brown sugar and flour in a bowl, add butter and rub in with fingertips until mixture resembles coarse breadcrumbs.

To make the cake, preheat the oven to 180°C (350°F). Sift flour, baking powder and salt into a mixing bowl. Place butter and sugar in a bowl and cream together. Add the eggs, and mix. Add the dry ingredients, alternating with sour cream, mixing well after each addition.

Pour the cake batter into a greased 23 cm (9 in) spring-form cake tin. Sprinkle with blueberries and topping mixture.

Bake the cake for 50 minutes or until a skewer comes out clean. Leave to cool in the tin for 10 minutes, then turn out onto a wire rack, topping-side-up.

Serve warm or at room temperature with fresh cream. Serves 8.

Mix up double quantities of this cookie dough, roll the excess into a log and keep in plastic wrap and foil in the freezer. To prepare, thaw slightly and slice into rounds 1 cm ($^{1}/_{2}$ in) thick before baking.

CHOCOLATE CHIP COOKIES

Like a genie from the bottle, the all-American mom is conjured by the aroma of choc-chip cookies baking. These imports are irresistible eaten fresh and still warm from the oven.

125 g (4 oz) unsalted butter, softened
1$^{1}/_{4}$ cups tightly packed brown sugar
1 teaspoon vanilla essence
1 egg, lightly beaten
1$^{1}/_{2}$ cups plain (all-purpose) flour
$^{1}/_{2}$ teaspoon baking powder
a pinch of salt
1$^{1}/_{2}$ cups chocolate bits

Preheat the oven to 180°C (350°F). Place butter and sugar in a bowl and beat until light and creamy. Add vanilla and egg and stir to combine. Stir in the sifted flour, baking powder and salt until just combined. Fold through chocolate chips.

Place spoonfuls of cookie mixture on a greased and lined baking tray, allowing room for spreading. Cook for 15–20 minutes, until they turn pale gold.

Allow to cool on the tray for 5 minutes before placing biscuits on a wire rack to cool further. Makes 16.

COCONUT AND PASSIONFRUIT SLICE

Passionfruit vines looped over garden fences turn exquisite flowers into tangy fruit. Sweet 'slices' cooked in lamington tins are a money-spinner at school fêtes all over Australia.

pastry	*filling*
125 g (4 oz) butter	4 eggs
1/2 cup caster (superfine) sugar	1 cup sugar
1 egg	1 cup shredded coconut
1 teaspoon vanilla essence	1/3 cup plain (all-purpose) flour
11/2 cup plain (all-purpose) flour	11/2 cups (12 fl oz) cream
1/2 teaspoon baking powder	160 ml (51/2 fl oz) coconut milk
a pinch of salt	juice and zest of 1 lemon
	1/2 cup (4 fl oz) passionfruit pulp

Preheat the oven to 180°C (350°F). To make the pastry, place butter and sugar in a bowl and beat until light and creamy. Add egg and vanilla essence and beat well. Add sifted flour, baking powder and salt, and stir until combined and the mixture forms a sticky dough.

Flour hands and press pastry evenly into the base of a greased and baking-paper-lined 23 x 23 cm (9 x 9 in) tin. Bake pastry base in the oven for 15 minutes.

To make filling, place eggs and sugar in a bowl and whisk until pale. Add coconut, flour, cream, coconut milk, lemon juice, zest and passionfruit pulp, and stir to combine.

Pour filling over pastry base in the tin. Bake for 35–40 minutes or until golden. Remove from the oven and allow to cool completely in the tin.

When cool, slice into squares. Makes 20 squares.

MANGO TART

In late spring city shoppers speculate about the coming mango season – a bumper crop means a glut of luscious fruit at bargain prices. Case-loads bought around Christmas can be devoured while hanging over the sink, or put to more elegant use.

1 quantity of sweet shortcrust pastry (see page 123)
1 cup (8 fl oz) milk
1 teaspoon vanilla essence
6 egg yolks
3/4 cup caster (superfine) sugar
3 tablespoons cornflour (cornstarch)
25 g (3/4 oz) butter
1/2 cup (4 fl oz) cream, lightly whipped
3 mangoes, peeled and sliced

On a lightly floured surface roll out the pastry to 3 mm (1/4 in) thick. Lightly press the pastry into a 23 cm (9 in) tart tin and freeze for 30 minutes. Preheat the oven to 180°C (350°F).

Remove pastry shell from the freezer and line with baking paper. Fill with baking weights or rice and bake the shell for 10 minutes. Remove paper and weights. Bake for a further 10 minutes, until dry, golden and crisp. Leave to cool.

Place milk in a saucepan over medium heat and heat until just before boiling point. Add vanilla. Remove from heat.

Place egg yolks and sugar in a bowl and beat until thick. Add the cornflour and hot milk and stir until smooth.

Return mixture to a clean saucepan over medium heat, stirring constantly with a wooden spoon for about 15 minutes, or until thickened.

Bring the custard to the boil, turn the heat down and cook for a further 2 minutes. Remove from heat and add butter, stirring to combine. Strain mixture into a bowl, lay plastic wrap on the surface and refrigerate until cold. Fold through cream.

Remove tart shell from the tin and place on a serving platter. Pour in custard and arrange mango slices decoratively on top. Serves 8.

ANZAC BISCUITS

These hero-sustaining treats are said to have been devised for sending in care packages to Australia and New Zealand Army Corps soldiers serving in World War I. They must be chewy, so be careful not to overcook them.

1 cup plain (all-purpose) flour
1 cup desiccated coconut
2/3 cup brown sugar
1 cup rolled oats
125 g (4 oz) butter
1 tablespoon golden syrup
1/2 teaspoon bicarbonate of soda (baking soda)
2 tablespoons boiling water

Preheat oven to 160°C (315°F). Place flour, coconut, sugar and oats in a bowl. Mix well.

Place butter and golden syrup in a saucepan over medium heat and melt.

Place bicarbonate of soda in a small bowl and add water. Stir to combine.

Add bicarbonate mixture to saucepan and stir. Pour over oat mixture and stir all ingredients together.

Roll teaspoonfuls of biscuit mixture into balls and place on a greased and lined baking tray, leaving room for spreading. Flatten each ball gently with a fork.

Bake biscuits for 15–20 minutes, or until biscuits are golden brown at the edges. Allow to cool slightly on trays before transferring to a wire rack. Makes 20.

UPSIDE-DOWN CAKE WITH APPLE AND CINNAMON

A magic inversion that brings buried treasure to the surface. One delicious variation substitutes sliced pears and chunks of ginger-in-syrup for apples.

topping
100 g (3¹/₃ oz) unsalted butter
4 large firm apples, peeled,
  cored and cut into 1 cm (¹/₂ in)
  slices
juice and zest of 1 lemon
1 cup caster (superfine) sugar
1 teaspoon vanilla essence

cake
100 g (3¹/₃ oz) unsalted butter, softened
1 cup caster (superfine) sugar
4 eggs, separated
1 teaspoon vanilla essence
1¹/₄ cups plain (all-purpose) flour
2 teaspoons baking powder
a pinch of salt
1 teaspoon ground cinnamon
pouring (single) cream, to serve

To make the topping, place the butter in a non-stick frying pan over medium heat and melt. Toss apples with lemon juice and zest in a bowl and add to butter. Cook apples gently for 3 minutes, stirring occasionally. Add sugar and vanilla and cook for 5 minutes longer.

Remove apples from the pan with a slotted spoon and arrange in the bottom of a greased and greaseproof-paper-lined 23 cm (9 in) spring-form cake tin.

Increase heat and boil remaining liquid in the pan for 5 more minutes until a rich caramel forms. Pour caramel over apples in the base of the tin.

To make the cake, preheat oven to 180°C (350°F). Place butter and sugar in a bowl and cream until light and fluffy. Add egg yolks one at a time, beating after each addition. Add vanilla. Gently fold in the sifted flour, baking powder, salt and cinnamon.

In a small, clean, dry bowl, beat egg whites until stiff. Fold through cake mixture with a large metal spoon. Spoon evenly over apples and caramel and smooth with a spatula.

Bake cake for 40 minutes or until a skewer inserted into the centre of the cake comes out clean.

Remove cake from the oven and leave in the tin for 5 minutes. Remove sides from the cake tin and place a large serving plate on top of cake. Turn cake over onto serving plate. Remove base and greaseproof paper.

Serve warm with cream. Serves 8–10.

GRANNY MAC'S SHORTBREAD

Shortbread is part of our Scottish/English heritage – the tartan-patterned tins were stashed out of reach of children until the teapot sat plump in its cozy, ready to pour.

2 cups plain (all-purpose) flour
1 teaspoon baking powder
1/2 cup caster (superfine) sugar
125 g (4 oz) butter, softened

1 egg, lightly beaten
1/3 cup jam
2 teaspoons ground cinnamon
icing sugar to serve

Sift flour, baking powder and sugar into a bowl. Add butter and rub in with fingertips until mixture resembles coarse breadcrumbs. Mix in 1–2 tablespoons of cold water to form a dough. Add egg and combine to form a stiff but workable dough. Roll out the dough on a sheet of greaseproof paper to form a 20 x 30 cm (8 x 12 in) rectangle. Spread jam evenly on the dough and sprinkle with cinnamon.

Roll up the dough swiss-roll style, peeling away the greaseproof paper as you go. Wrap the roll in plastic wrap and refrigerate for 30 minutes. Preheat oven to 180°C (350°F). Remove dough from the refrigerator and cut into slices 1 cm (1/2 in) thick. Place shortbreads on a lined baking tray and bake for 15–20 minutes or until lightly browned. Cool on wire racks and sprinkle with icing sugar. Makes 24.

CHOCOLATE-DIPPED SHORTBREAD

1/3 cup icing (confectioners') sugar
250 g (8 oz) unsalted butter, softened
1 teaspoon vanilla essence
11/2 cups plain (all-purpose) flour
1/2 cup cornflour (cornstarch)
a pinch of salt
125 g (4 oz) good-quality dark chocolate, in small pieces

Place sugar and butter in a bowl and beat until just combined. Add vanilla, sifted flours and salt, and mix until a dough forms. Mould the dough into a log 6 cm (21/2 in) in diameter, wrap in plastic wrap and chill for 30 minutes. Preheat oven to 180°C (350°F).

Remove dough from refrigerator and cut into 1 cm (1/2 in) slices. Place rounds on greased and lined baking trays and bake for 20–25 minutes, or until golden brown. Remove shortbread onto wire racks and cool completely.

Place chocolate in a heatproof bowl resting over a saucepan of hot water over low heat and heat until chocolate has melted. Dip shortbread into chocolate and allow to cool on a wire rack placed over a tray to catch any drips. Makes 16.

NECTARINE AND PLUM TART

This is an adaptation of a Stephanie Alexander recipe for quince tarts. You could substitute shortcrust pastry from the supermarket to speed preparation, and the burnt butter topping is wonderful just drizzled over poached pears or peaches.

1 quantity sweet shortcrust pastry (below)
2 nectarines, stoned and cut into 6 pieces
2 plums, stoned and cut into 6 pieces
3 eggs
1/2 cup caster (superfine) sugar
2 tablespoons plain (all-purpose) flour
90 g (3 oz) unsalted butter, melted and lightly browned

Roll out the pastry on a lightly floured surface until it is 3 mm (1/4 in) thick. Gently press pastry into a 23 cm (9 in) tart tin and freeze for 30 minutes.

Preheat the oven to 180°C (350°F). Remove pastry shell from the freezer and line with baking paper. Distribute baking weights or rice on the surface of the paper and bake the shell for 10 minutes. Remove paper and weights and bake for a further 10 minutes, until dry, golden and crisp. Leave to cool.

Arrange fruit, skin-side-down, in pastry case.

Place eggs and sugar in a bowl and whisk until thick and pale. Add flour and butter and gently combine.

Pour filling evenly over fruit. Bake for 30–40 minutes, or until golden and set in the centre. Serves 8.

SWEET SHORTCRUST PASTRY

2 cups plain (all-purpose) flour
1/4 cup icing (confectioners') sugar, sifted
a pinch of salt
180 g (6 oz) unsalted butter

Place flour, sugar and salt in a bowl. Add butter and rub through with fingertips until the mixture resembles coarse breadcrumbs.

Add 3 tablespoons of cold water and cut in with a knife until the dough comes together in a ball.

Wrap pastry in plastic wrap, and refrigerate for 30 minutes.

LUNCH DRINKS + NIBBLES

Inviting friends for afternoon drinks takes the pressure off for a traditional dinner party. Bend your usual schedule around small meals with big flavour.

GINGER PICKLED SALMON ON WITLOF

300 g (10 oz) salmon fillets, skin removed and cut into 5 mm dice
1/3 cup (2 3/4 fl oz) pickling liquid (below)
1 tablespoon Japanese pickled ginger, finely chopped
4 heads baby witlof, leaves separated
2 tablespoons finely chopped chives

Place salmon, pickling liquid and ginger in a bowl and stir to combine. Leave to marinate in the refrigerator for 2 hours. Drain and discard excess liquid.

Arrange witlof leaves on a serving platter and spoon a teaspoon of salmon mixture on each leaf. Sprinkle with chives. Serves 8–10.

PICKLING LIQUID

1 cup (8 fl oz) Japanese seasoned rice vinegar
2 tablespoons sugar
1 teaspoon salt
2 tablespoons grated fresh ginger
1 fresh chilli, sliced
1 teaspoon Szechuan peppercorns

Warm the vinegar, sugar, salt, ginger, chilli and peppercorns in a small saucepan over medium heat until the sugar dissolves. Allow to cool.

ICED MINT AND GINGER TEA

1 litre (32 fl oz) boiling water
1 cup mint leaves
1/3 cup peeled and sliced fresh ginger
3 tablespoons sugar
ice
mint sprigs to serve

Pour boiling water over mint leaves, ginger and sugar in a jug. Stir until sugar dissolves. Allow to cool. Refrigerate and serve on ice with sprigs of mint. Serves 4.

SPICY PRAWN CAKES

500 g (1 lb) green (raw) prawns,
  peeled
1 tablespoon fish sauce
1 green chilli, chopped
2 cloves garlic, crushed
1/2 teaspoon turmeric
1/2 teaspoon white pepper
2 tablespoons chopped coriander
  (cilantro) roots and leaves
3 spring (green) onions, finely sliced
plain (all-purpose) flour
1 cup (8 fl oz) vegetable oil

to serve
coriander (cilantro) dipping
  sauce (below)
coriander (cilantro) sprigs (optional)

Place prawns, fish sauce, chilli, garlic, turmeric, pepper and coriander in a food processor and process to a paste. Fold in spring onions. Shape prawn mixture into little balls, 3 cm (11/4 in) in diameter, and roll in flour to coat lightly.

Heat vegetable oil in a deep frying pan until hot. Add prawn balls and shallow fry until golden. Remove with a slotted spoon and drain on paper towels.

Serve with dipping sauce, coriander sprigs if desired and toothpicks or tiny cocktail forks. Makes 8–10.

CORIANDER DIPPING SAUCE

3 cloves garlic
2 large green chillies, seeded and roughly chopped
1 tablespoon palm sugar
4 tablespoons lime juice
3 teaspoons fish sauce
1 cup roughly chopped coriander (cilantro)

Place all the ingredients in a blender with 3 tablespoons of water and blend until combined. Pour into a small serving bowl.

VIETNAMESE LEMONADE

per serve
1 teaspoon caster (superfine) sugar
1/2 cup ice

2 tablespoons lemon juice
slice of lemon
mineral water

Place sugar in the bottom of a tall glass. Add ice, lemon juice, the slice of lemon and top up with mineral water. Serve with a long spoon and a straw.

DINNER

Twilight, Sydney Opera House Forecourt,
Bennelong Point

SYDNEY MEETS FOR DRINKS

SIDLING THROUGH CONVERSATION TO THE MOST ATTRACTIVE DINNER OPTION. MOBILE PHONES HUM AND AAH OVER BOOKINGS. INVITATIONS TO DINNER AT HOME HAVE A HIGH VALUE: LAMB TAGINE, ROAST CHICKEN WITH TOMATO SALAD OR SEAFOOD STEW ARE DISHES EASILY MADE IN QUANTITIES TO SHARE. FOLLOW UP WITH CARAMEL-DRIZZLED BAKED FRUIT IN SEASON. BUT MOST EVENINGS, IT'S A RUSH FOR THE BUS, OR THE TRAIN'S OPEN-AND-SHUT REFRAIN, AND ANXIOUS RECKONINGS OF WHAT'S IN THE FRIDGE. IF YOU HAVEN'T MARINATED THE BEEF, IT MIGHT BE A NICOISE SALAD WITH TUNA FROM THE CAN, OR FRIED RICE WITH EGG AND PEAS, AND MAYBE A BACI CHOCOLATE ON THE WAY TO BED – AN ITALIAN KISS GOODNIGHT.

SKEWERED SWORDFISH WITH CRISPY COLESLAW

Swordfish is the steak of the sea – it's meaty. Skewering it in chunks makes it accessible and helps cook it evenly. A crunchy slaw is the perfect clean-flavoured accompaniment.

2 tablespoons lime juice

2 cloves garlic, sliced

2 tablespoons olive oil

1/2 teaspoon sea salt

freshly ground black pepper

2 x 2 cm thick swordfish steaks, cut into 3 pieces on the diagonal

1 cup Chinese cabbage, finely sliced

1/2 cup snowpeas, finely sliced on the diagonal

1 stick celery, cut into thin 4 cm long batons

2 spring (green) onions, finely sliced on the diagonal

4 fresh kaffir lime leaves (optional)

1/4 cup (2 fl oz) soy dressing (below)

1 tablespoon toasted sesame seeds

Soak 2 wooden skewers in water for 1 hour.

Place lime juice, garlic, oil, salt and pepper in a bowl and stir to combine. Add swordfish pieces and leave to marinate for at least 1 hour in the refrigerator.

Meanwhile, place cabbage, snowpeas, celery and spring onion in a bowl and toss to combine. Cover and refrigerate.

Assemble by alternating three pieces of swordfish with 2 lime leaves on each skewer. Divide coleslaw between 2 plates, drizzle with soy dressing and sprinkle with sesame seeds.

Heat a large non-stick frying pan over high heat and cook each swordfish skewer for 2 minutes. Turn and cook for another 2 minutes. Remove from heat and place a skewer on top of each plate of coleslaw. Serves 2.

SOY DRESSING

1 tablespoon sesame oil	2 tablespoons sugar
1/2 cup (4 fl oz) soy sauce	3 tablespoons lime juice
1 1/2 tablespoons balsamic vinegar	2 chillies, chopped

Place sesame oil, soy sauce, balsamic vinegar, sugar, lime juice and chillies in a bowl and whisk to combine.

PARMESAN VEAL SCHNITZEL WITH CREAMED POTATOES

This is real comfort food, as evidenced by the fact that we can't take it off the menu without uproar from the regulars at bills. I like the schnitzel with a rocket or tomato salad, to cut the richness – but then, a lot of people just order anything with mash.

8 veal escalopes
1 cup fresh breadcrumbs
1 cup finely grated Parmesan cheese
1/2 cup parsley
2 tablespoons finely chopped thyme
1 teaspoon sea salt
freshly ground black pepper
1/4 cup (2 fl oz) milk
2 eggs
1 cup plain (all-purpose) flour
1/2 cup (4 fl oz) olive oil

to serve
creamed potatoes (below)
lemon wedges
rocket (arugula) leaves

Place veal escalopes on a board and flatten with a mallet.

Place breadcrumbs, Parmesan cheese, parsley, thyme, salt and pepper in a bowl and mix well. Place milk and eggs in a bowl and beat lightly together. Place flour in a bowl.

Dip veal first in the flour, then egg wash and finally in breadcrumb mixture. Continue until all veal is coated.

Heat olive oil in a large non-stick frying pan over medium heat. Place veal in frying pan in a single layer, being careful not to crowd, and cook for 2 minutes until golden brown on one side. Turn veal and cook for a further 2 minutes. Remove from pan and keep warm until all the veal escalopes are cooked.

Serve with creamed potatoes, lemon wedges and rocket leaves. Serves 4.

CREAMED POTATOES

800 g (1 lb 10 oz) potatoes suitable for mashing (such as pontiacs)
1 cup (8 fl oz) cream
75 g (21/2 oz) butter
1 teaspoon sea salt

Place potatoes in boiling water and cook until tender. Remove from heat, drain and mash potatoes in saucepan. Place cream and butter in a small saucepan over medium heat until hot (don't allow to boil), and the butter has melted.

Beat cream mixture into potatoes with a wooden spoon until smooth. Season with salt to taste.

ROAST CHICKEN WITH YOGHURT GARLIC SAUCE

Crispy-skinned chicken, tangy tomato and a garlic-redolent middle-eastern sauce – my adaptation of a classic Roger Verge recipe. Sun-soaked Sydney days end easily in meals like this, with fresh bread to mop up the juices.

1 x 1.5 kg (3 lb) chicken
sea salt
freshly ground black pepper
1 onion, finely sliced
2 lemons
1 tablespoon chopped oregano
5 tablespoons olive oil

to serve
tomato salad (see left)
yoghurt garlic sauce (below)

Serve this chicken with a marinated-tomato salad. Quarter small, ripe tomatoes and sprinkle with sea salt, red wine vinegar and olive oil. Marinate for an hour before draining, and mix with chopped flat-leaf parsley and a drizzle of olive oil.

Remove the backbone of the chicken: place the chicken, breast-side-down, on a cutting board or plate; using a sharp pair of kitchen scissors, cut through the meat and bones on either side of the back bone. Cut off the wing tips. Make a small incision at the joint where the drumstick meets the thigh. Flatten out the chicken with your hands. Season on both sides with salt and pepper.

Spread the onion on the bottom of a baking dish and place the chicken skin-side-up on the bed of onions. Cut one of the lemons into fine slices and arrange over the chicken. Sprinkle with oregano and 2 tablespoons of the olive oil. Cover and leave for 4 hours.

Preheat the oven to 250°C (500°F). Remove chicken from marinade, transfer to a baking tray and place under a very hot grill for 10 minutes or until chicken is golden brown. Turn chicken over, drizzle with another tablespoon of olive oil and cook on the other side until golden brown.

Return chicken to baking dish with onions, skin-side-up, and drizzle with 2 tablespoons of olive oil. Bake for 15 minutes. Squeeze the juice of the remaining lemon over the chicken and cook for a further 10 minutes, or until chicken is cooked. Serve with tomato salad and yoghurt garlic sauce. Serves 4.

YOGHURT GARLIC SAUCE

2 cloves garlic, crushed
1/4 teaspoon sea salt

1 cup (8 fl oz) yoghurt

Crush garlic with salt and mix with yoghurt. Leave for 1 hour for flavours to combine.

MOROCCAN LAMB TAGINE

Tagines added spice to Australian cooking in the early Nineties. Suddenly cinnamon entered the savoury and the scent of cardamom rose from ovens all over Sydney. It's the kind of dish that tastes better still if refrigerated for a day before skimming off the fat and reheating.

1 tablespoon olive oil
8 small frenched lamb shanks
1 Spanish onion, chopped
2 cloves garlic, sliced
1 tablespoon grated ginger
1 teaspoon chilli powder
1 teaspoon turmeric
1 teaspoon ground cumin
1 teaspoon cardamom pods
1 cinnamon stick
2 tablespoons grated palm sugar
4 teaspoons fish sauce
4 large ripe tomatoes, roughly chopped
4 kaffir lime leaves
2 cups (16 fl oz) chicken stock or water
2 potatoes, unpeeled and chopped
1 sweet potato, unpeeled and chopped

When making the couscous, use a whisk to mix the grains and water. This gives a fluffier consistency than just stirring with a fork.

Preheat oven to 160°C (315°F). Heat oil in a frying pan over a high heat. Add lamb shanks and cook for 2 minutes on each side, or until they are well browned. Remove lamb and place in a baking dish.

Reduce heat to medium and add onion to the pan. Cook for 5 minutes, stirring occasionally, until onion is translucent. Add garlic and ginger and cook for 1 minute longer, then add chilli powder, turmeric, cumin, cardamom and cinnamon. Cook for 2 minutes, stirring constantly. Add sugar, fish sauce, chopped tomatoes, lime leaves and stock, and bring to the boil. Remove from heat.

Add potatoes and sweet potato to the baking dish with the lamb, and pour the sauce over the top. Cover with foil and bake for 2 hours, or until the lamb falls away from the bone.

Serve with steamed couscous or rice. Serves 4.

BARBECUED WHOLE FISH WITH FRESH HERB RELISH

Clean-flavoured, slightly sweet, with firm texture – barramundi from the northern fisheries of Australia is enhanced by the slight smoky charring of barbecue cooking.

2 whole barramundi, cleaned and
    dried, scored on both sides
    with three diagonal incisions
1/2 cup (4 fl oz) extra virgin olive oil
1 red chilli, chopped
2 cloves garlic, crushed
sea salt
freshly ground black pepper

to serve
lemon wedges
fresh herb relish (below)

Place olive oil, chilli, garlic, salt and pepper in a blender and process until smooth.

Rub chilli oil inside and over fish and leave to marinate for 1 hour.

Drain excess oil from fish and place the barramundi in a hinged fish grill, if you have one (this makes fish easier to turn on the barbecue, but is not essential).

Heat barbecue until flames have died down and coals are white hot. Place fish on the barbecue and cook for 3–4 minutes on each side.

Remove fish from the barbecue and serve with lemon wedges, lots of freshly ground black pepper and fresh herb relish on the side. Serves 2–4.

FRESH HERB RELISH

2 cups parsley, roughly chopped
2 cups basil leaves, roughly chopped
1/4 cup mint leaves
1/2 cup chopped spring (green) onions
1 tablespoon capers
2 anchovies
1/2 cup (4 fl oz) extra virgin olive oil

1 tablespoon lemon juice
sea salt
freshly ground black pepper
2 cloves garlic, crushed

Place all ingredients in a blender or food processor and process until a smooth sauce forms. Serve in a bowl and let each guest drizzle their own.

Never keep tomatoes in the fridge
(it alters both texture and flavour).
They improve with age in a bowl
on the kitchen counter.

FRESH TOMATO PASTA

We'd been complaining about the state of modern tomatoes for years, and then came the return to vine-ripened reds. So good you can eat them like apples – or let hot spaghetti stir up the fresh aroma.

1 kg (2 lb) vine-ripened tomatoes
1 tablespoon sea salt
1/2 cup (4 fl oz) extra virgin olive oil
2 tablespoons red wine vinegar
juice and zest of 1 lemon
2 cloves garlic, crushed
1 small red chilli, finely chopped
freshly ground black pepper
300 g (10 oz) spaghetti
1 cup lightly packed basil leaves, torn

to serve
Parmigiano Reggiano

Score a cross in the base of each tomato. Place tomatoes in a large bowl and pour boiling water over them. Drain after 10 seconds, then peel the skin away from the cross. Halve the tomatoes, and press halves to squeeze out seeds and excess juice. Chop tomato flesh roughly, place in a sieve over a bowl and sprinkle with sea salt. Leave to drain for half an hour.

Place drained tomatoes, olive oil, vinegar, lemon juice and zest, garlic, chilli and pepper in a bowl and stir. Leave for 20 minutes, for flavours to combine.

Cook the spaghetti in rapidly boiling salted water according to manufacturer's instructions. Drain well. Toss through tomatoes with freshly torn basil leaves, and serve with freshly shaved Parmigiano Reggiano. Serves 4.

GRILLED BEEF WITH BLACKBEAN

Blackbean sauce developed a dubious reputation in the days when Australian-Chinese restaurants catered to local palates. This more authentic recipe, from chef Kylie Kwong, gives our best-quality fillet steak a velvety texture, creating a local sensation from Chinese tradition.

marinade
1/2 cup shao hsing wine
4 tablespoons oyster sauce
2 tablespoons caster (superfine) sugar
2 tablespoons kecap manis
1 tablespoon sesame oil
1 tablespoon fish sauce

4 fillet steaks
3 tablespoons vegetable oil

2 cloves garlic, crushed
2 tablespoons salted blackbeans,
　rinsed, drained and lightly mashed
　with a fork
1 tablespoon dark soy sauce
1 teaspoon sugar
1 tablespoon shao hsing wine
1 teaspoon sesame oil

to serve
asparagus spears, lightly steamed

To make the marinade, place wine, oyster sauce, caster sugar, kecap manis, sesame oil and fish sauce in a bowl and stir to combine.

Add beef to marinade and turn several times to coat and cover. Refrigerate overnight. Drain.

Heat 2 tablespoons of the oil in a non-stick frying pan over high heat. Sear steaks for 2 minutes each side. Remove steaks from the pan and set aside.

Heat remaining oil in the pan, add garlic and fry for 30 seconds, add blackbeans, soy, sugar, wine and 2 tablespoons of water. Bring to the boil, lower heat and simmer for 5 minutes. Stir in sesame oil and remove from heat.

to serve Slice fillet steaks finely and pour sauce over individual portions. Arrange lightly steamed asparagus spears on top. Serves 4.

FRIED RICE WITH EGG AND FRESH PEAS

A recipe to soothe the children and fortify adults for the coming week. Fried rice cooked in the northern Chinese style is my Sunday-night recommendation, served with soy sauce and chilli on the side.

3 1/2 tablespoons vegetable oil
2 eggs, lightly beaten
3 cups cooked white rice, preferably cold
1 teaspoon salt
1/2 cup fresh peas, blanched
1/2 cup spring (green) onions, finely sliced
sweet chilli sauce, to serve

Place a wok over high heat. Add 1 1/2 tablespooons of oil and reduce heat after a minute. Add eggs, allow to cook for 20 seconds and scramble briefly. When eggs are half-cooked, remove them to a bowl.

Clean the wok with a paper towel and return it to high heat. Add 2 tablespoons of oil. Add rice and stir-fry for 3 minutes. If dry, add a little more oil.

Add salt and peas and stir-fry for 30 seconds more. Return eggs to the pan, add spring onions and toss gently together.

Spoon into individual bowls and top with sweet chillli sauce. Serves 2.

I have a weakness for bottled Thai sweet chilli sauce. Mix it with a little fresh lime juice and some chopped coriander (cilantro), to cut the sweetness.

SPICY FRIED CHICKEN

This recipe is a tribute to tales I've heard of Balinese chicken dishes. Frying can easily result in dry chicken meat but, in this case, the coconut milk keeps it moist and juicy. Delicious cold, it makes great picnic food.

1 cup (8 fl oz) coconut milk
3 kaffir lime leaves, or zest of 1 lime
2 Asian red shallots, roughly chopped
3 cloves garlic, crushed
1 x 2 cm (3/4 in) piece galangal (or ginger) root, sliced
3 green chillies, roughly chopped
1 teaspoon turmeric
1 tablespoon salt
1 x 1.5 kg (3 lb) chicken, cut into 16 pieces
vegetable oil for frying

to serve
sweet chilli sauce
cucumber slices
coriander (cilantro) sprigs

Place coconut milk, lime leaves (or zest), shallots, garlic, galangal root (or ginger), chillies, turmeric, salt and 2½ cups (20 fl oz) of water in large saucepan and bring to a simmer over medium heat. Add chicken and cook for 20 minutes or until chicken is tender and just cooked. Remove chicken from saucepan and leave to cool on a wire rack.

Heat oil to 3 cm (1¼ in) in a wok or deep frying pan on high heat. Cook the chicken in batches, being careful not to overcrowd, until golden. Drain on paper towels. Serve with sweet chilli sauce, cucumber slices and coriander sprigs. Serves 4.

LAMB CUTLETS WITH SKORDALIA AND PARSLEY SALAD

Australian spring lamb benefits from Greek influences: a pungent salad balances the sizzling fat of the cutlets and the richness of garlic.

1 tablespoon tomato paste
1 tablespoon harissa paste (optional)
3 tablespoons olive oil
2 garlic cloves, crushed with salt
freshly ground black pepper
4 x 4 cutlet racks of lamb

to serve
skordalia (below)
parsley salad (below)

Place tomato paste, harissa, olive oil, garlic and pepper in a bowl and stir to combine. Place lamb in a shallow dish and pour over marinade. Leave to marinate in the fridge for at least 1 hour, or overnight if possible.

Preheat the oven to 220°C (425°F). Heat an ovenproof frying pan until very hot. Place lamb racks, fat-side-down, in the pan for 2 minutes. Turn racks, with fat-side-up, place in the oven for 10 minutes. Remove from the oven and allow the lamb to rest in the pan for a further 10 minutes.

Slice racks into cutlets. Serve with skordalia and parsley salad. Serves 4.

SKORDALIA

3 potatoes, unpeeled
4 cloves garlic
a pinch of salt

1 tablespoon lemon juice
3/4 cup (6 fl oz) olive oil
1/4 cup (2 fl oz) milk

Cook potatoes in boiling water, peel and chop roughly. Place potatoes, garlic, salt and lemon juice in a food processor and begin blending. Add olive oil in a thin stream until all the oil is incorporated. Add milk slowly until combined. Serve at room temperature.

PARSLEY SALAD

2 white onions, finely sliced
1 teaspoon sea salt
1/2 cup parsley

1/4 cup mint leaves
1 teaspoon sumac
1 tablespoon olive oil

Place onions and salt in a bowl and toss to combine. Leave for 5 minutes. Rinse and dry the onions and mix with the parsley, mint and sumac. Drizzle with olive oil. Serve immediately.

WARM POACHED CHICKEN WITH ONION RICE AND FRESH GINGER RELISH

This dish is based on a Chinese Hainan recipe. Buy the best-quality chicken, such as a Kangaroo Island bird, because the cooking method really allows its flavour to shine through.

1 x 1.5 kg (3 lb) chicken, excess
    fat removed
1 bunch coriander (cilantro), including
    roots (reserve leaves for sauce)
3 spring (green) onions, chopped
1 teaspoon black peppercorns
2 tablespoons salt
500 g (1 lb) long-grain rice
1 tablespoon vegetable oil

1 tablespoon sesame oil
1 tablespoon crushed garlic
1 tablespoon grated ginger
1 onion, finely sliced
to serve
coriander (cilantro) sprigs
fresh ginger relish (below)
cucumber

Place chicken in a large saucepan and add coriander roots and stems, spring onions, peppercorns, salt and 2 litres (64 fl oz) of water. Bring to the boil.

Reduce heat to a bare simmer, cover saucepan and continue to simmer for 25 minutes. Remove from heat and leave the chicken in the pot for a further 40 minutes, without lifting the lid.

Wash rice until water runs clear. Heat the oils in a medium saucepan over low heat and add garlic, ginger and onion. Cook for 15 minutes or until onion is soft. Add rice to the pan and stir-fry for 3 minutes until grains are well-coated with oil. Increase heat to medium-high, add 1 litre of chicken liquid to rice and bring to the boil. Reduce heat to a simmer and cook, covered, for 15 minutes. Remove from heat and leave for 10 minutes without lifting the lid. Before serving, season with salt and pepper.

Remove chicken from the saucepan and cut into serving-size pieces. Decorate with sprigs of coriander. Serve with onion rice, fresh ginger relish and a bowl of peeled and sliced cucumber. Serves 6.

FRESH GINGER RELISH

2 tablespoons ginger, cut into matchsticks
8 spring (green) onions, finely sliced
1/4 cup (2 fl oz) vegetable oil
salt and pepper

In a mortar and pestle, lightly bruise the ginger and spring onions. Heat the oil in a pan until smoking and pour over ginger mixture in a heat-proof bowl. Season with salt and pepper. Allow to cool before serving.

Good-quality dried pasta goes well with fresh-tasting sauces like this, where home-made pasta would be too heavy.

PRAWN AND CHILLI LINGUINE

Peak prawn season at the Sydney markets used to be in spring and summer and, although farming has made them constantly available, most locals still associate them with warm-weather festivities.

250 g (8 oz) linguine

4 tablespoons olive oil

10 green (raw) prawns, peeled and
  deveined, with tails intact

sea salt

freshly ground black pepper

2 cloves garlic, crushed

2 small red chillies, finely chopped

25 g (3/4 oz) butter

50 g (1 1/2 oz) baby rocket (arugula), washed and dried

to serve

a few extra rocket (arugula) leaves

Cook linguine in rapidly boiling salted water according to manufacturer's instructions. Drain well.

Heat oil in a large non-stick frying pan over medium heat. Add prawns, season with salt and pepper, and cook for 1 minute. Add garlic and chillies and cook for another minute. Add butter and reduce heat to low. Add the rocket and cooked linguine. Toss linguine through the sauce until it is coated.

To serve, divide the pasta between 2 bowls. Decorate with extra rocket leaves and a wedge of lemon. Serves 2.

BARBECUED BUGS WITH TOMATO GREMOLATA

Balmain or Moreton Bay are the varieties of bug – a small lobster-like crustacean – most frequently found at Sydney's fishmarket. The aroma of bugs cooking is the winner in the one-upmanship of barbecue waftings waged over backyard fences.

1/2 cup (4 fl oz) extra virgin olive oil
500 g (1 lb) ripe tomatoes, peeled, seeded and cut into 5 mm dice
2 tablespoons very finely chopped parsley
2 spring (green) onions, finely sliced
juice and zest of 2 limes
1 teaspoon red wine vinegar
1 green chilli, finely chopped
sea salt
freshly ground black pepper
20 Balmain or Moreton Bay bugs, cleaned and halved, shells on, with intestinal
   tracts removed
flatleaf parsley for garnish

Gently warm olive oil in a saucepan on low heat.

Place remaining ingredients, except the bugs, in a bowl. Add warmed oil and stir to combine. Pour gremolata into a serving bowl.

Heat the barbecue until flames have died down and coals are white hot. Place bugs on the barbecue and cook for 10 minutes or until the shells are very red.

Remove the bugs from the shell. Garnish with parsley and cracked black pepper. Serve with the tomato gremolata. Serves 4.

GRILLED QUAIL WITH COUSCOUS SALAD

Using a coal-fired barbecue adds smoky flavours to this North African-inspired dish.

3 tablespoons olive oil	freshly ground black pepper
2 cloves garlic, crushed	4 quails, boned and flattened
1/2 teaspoon ground coriander	(get your butcher to do this)
1/2 teaspoon ground cumin	*to serve*
1/2 teaspoon paprika	couscous salad (below)
1 teaspoon sea salt	chilli mint harissa (below)

Mix together the olive oil, garlic, spices, salt and pepper. Place quails in a shallow dish and rub with marinade. Leave for at least 1 hour, or overnight if possible.

Preheat oven to 220°C (425°F). Heat an ovenproof frying pan over high heat until very hot. Sear the quails, skin-side-down, in the pan for 2 minutes. Turn the quails over and cook for a further 2 minutes. Bake in the oven for 5 minutes. Remove from the oven and leave in the pan for a further 10 minutes. Serve on couscous salad drizzled with harissa and pan juices. Serves 4.

COUSCOUS SALAD

2 tablespoons olive oil	1/2 telegraph cucumber, peeled,
2 tablespoons lemon juice	seeded and chopped
sea salt	into 1 cm (1/2 in) dice
freshly ground black pepper	2 spring (green) onions, finely sliced
125 g (4 oz) packet couscous, cooked	2 tablespoons finely chopped mint
and cooled	3 tablespoons finely chopped parsley
2 tomatoes, seeded and	
chopped into 1 cm (1/2 in) dice	

Whisk together olive oil, lemon juice, salt and pepper. Place couscous, tomatoes, cucumber, spring onions, mint and parsley in a bowl and mix well, making sure that couscous is completely broken up. Pour dressing over salad and mix again.

CHILLI MINT HARISSA

1/2 cup roasted, peeled and	1/2 teaspoon sea salt
chopped red capsicum (pepper)	3 red chillies, chopped
1/2 cup roasted, chopped tomatoes	3 tablespoons olive oil
1/2 teaspoon sugar	1/4 cup finely chopped mint

In a blender, combine all ingredients, except mint, until smooth. Pour into a bowl, add mint and stir before serving.

To make garlic toasts, preheat the oven to 200°C (400°F). Blend a quarter of a cup of extra virgin olive oil with two cloves of garlic. Cut half a baguette into thin slices. Arrange in one layer on a baking tray and brush each slice with the garlic oil. Sprinkle generously with salt and pepper and bake until brown and crisp.

SEAFOOD STEW

This is an easy, satisfying one-pot dish for those Sydney nights when the wind seems to be blowing cold off the Snowy Mountains. To make it even more hearty you can add boiled and sliced baby potatoes.

¼ cup (2 fl oz) extra virgin olive oil
1 small onion, finely chopped
3 cloves garlic, crushed
1 small red chilli, finely chopped
3 tablespoons finely chopped parsley
½ cup (4 fl oz) white wine
400 g (13 oz) can Italian chopped
   tomatoes
3–4 vine-ripened tomatoes, chopped
1 teaspoon orange zest
12 mussels in their shells,
   cleaned and bearded, any
   open mussels discarded

24 pippis, in their shells, cleaned
12 green (raw) prawns, peeled and
   deveined, with tails intact
12 scallops, cleaned and deveined
sea salt
freshly ground black pepper
to serve

3 tablespoons finely chopped
   parsley
garlic toasts (see above)

Heat olive oil in a large deep frying pan over medium heat. Add onion and cook for 5 minutes or until translucent. Add garlic and chilli and cook 1 minute longer. Add the parsley and stir for 20 seconds, then add wine and bring to the boil. Add canned and fresh tomatoes, and zest. Reduce to low heat and cook for 25 minutes.

   Add mussels and pippis, stir, return heat to medium-high and cover the pan. Remove lid after 2 minutes and stir. Add prawns and scallops as soon as mussels and pippis begin to open. Cook for 2 minutes longer until prawns and scallops are opaque. Discard any unopened mussels or pippis.

   Spoon stew into shallow bowls and sprinkle with extra parsley. Serve with garlic toasts on the side. Serves 4.

BAKED SNAPPER WITH LEMON-ROASTED POTATOES AND FENNEL CHILLI RELISH

Fish and fennel are a pleasing combination. The fennel season makes this a winter recipe, with a little extra heat from the chilli to warm the evening.

2 x 750 g (1½ lb) snappers,
  cleaned and dried
sea salt
2 fennel tops, sliced
1 lemon, finely sliced
¼ cup (2 fl oz) olive oil
freshly ground black pepper

to serve
lemon-roasted potatoes (below)
fennel chilli relish (below)

Preheat the oven to 180°C (350°F). Score 2–3 deep cuts in each side of the fish at the thickest part. Rub the cavities of the snapper with salt and place fennel tops and lemon inside. Rub the fish with one-third of the olive oil.

Place the remaining oil in a baking tray and lay the fish on top. Bake for 20–25 minutes. Spoon fennel chilli relish on top of the fish and grind over black pepper before serving. Serves 4.

LEMON-ROASTED POTATOES

750 g (1½ lb) kipfler potatoes,
unpeeled and sliced in half lengthways
1 lemon, finely sliced
2 bay leaves (optional)
sea salt

freshly ground black pepper
3 cloves garlic, unpeeled,
  crushed with the side of a knife
¼ cup (2 fl oz) olive oil

Preheat the oven to 180°C (350°F). Place all ingredients in a bowl and toss until potatoes are coated in oil. Spread in a baking dish and cover with foil. Bake for 20 minutes. Remove foil and bake a further 20 minutes or until golden brown. Serve with freshly ground black pepper.

FENNEL CHILLI RELISH

1 fennel bulb, finely chopped
  to 5 mm dice
2 red chillies, finely chopped
juice of 1 lemon

¼ cup parsley, finely chopped
3 tablespoons extra virgin olive oil
sea salt
freshly ground black pepper

Place all ingredients in a bowl and stir to combine.

POACHED SALMON WITH GREEN-BEAN SALAD AND TOMATO AND ANCHOVY DRESSING

A recipe essential to the Sydney commuter's repertoire – it can be prepared in half an hour when the trek home has driven you to food-craving distraction. Substitute chunks of canned tuna if the fish shop is closed.

2 tablespoons salt

1 teaspoon white peppercorns

2 bay leaves

1 baby fennel, finely sliced,
  top reserved

4 x 175 g (5½ oz) salmon fillets, skin off

300 g (10 oz) green beans, steamed

200 g (6½ oz) sugarsnap peas, steamed

to serve

tomato and anchovy dressing (below)

Place the salt, peppercorns, bay leaves and fennel top in a large deep frying pan with 5 cups (40 fl oz) of water and bring to the boil. Cook for 5 minutes then remove from the heat. Add the salmon, cover and leave for 15 minutes. Remove the fish from the stock and break into large pieces.

   Serve on a bed of steamed green beans, sugarsnap peas and sliced fennel, with the tomato and anchovy dressing drizzled over the top. Serves 4.

TOMATO AND ANCHOVY DRESSING

3 vine-ripened tomatoes,
  finely chopped

2 anchovies, finely chopped

1 onion, finely chopped

2 tablespoons lemon juice

¼ cup (2 fl oz) olive oil

½ cup basil, chopped

Place all ingredients in a bowl and mix to combine.

APPLE AND RHUBARB PIE

Perfume a winter afternoon with a just-baked pie. Tart Granny Smiths are the best choice for this recipe.

1 kg (2 lb) green apples, peeled, cored and finely sliced
juice and zest of 1 lemon
50 g (1 3/4 oz) butter, cut into small pieces
300 g (10 oz) rhubarb, chopped
300 g (10 oz) caster (superfine) sugar
2 tablespoons plain (all-purpose) flour
1 teaspoon ground cinnamon
1 quantity shortcrust pastry (below)
2 egg yolks, lightly beaten
2 tablespoons caster (superfine) sugar for sprinkling

Toss the apples with the lemon juice and zest. Melt the butter in a large frypan over medium heat. Add the apples and cook for 5 minutes, or until softened slightly. Add the rhubarb and the sugar and cook for 1 minute further. Add the flour and cinnamon, and stir gently to combine. Allow to cool.

Place half the pastry on a lightly floured surface and roll out until 4 mm thick. Lightly press into a 23 cm (9 in) pie tin and refrigerate while the filling is cooling.

Spread apples and rhubarb evenly in the pie shell.

Preheat the oven to 200°C (400°F). Moisten edges of pastry base with egg yolk. Roll out remaining pastry on a lightly floured surface until 4 mm (1/4 in) thick. Cover pie with the rolled pastry. Trim, press the edges of the pie firmly together and crimp the outer rim with your fingertips. Make incisions in the top of the pie with a sharp knife. Brush with remaining egg yolk and sprinkle with extra caster sugar.

Bake the pie for 1 hour until the crust is golden brown. (If crust starts to brown too quickly, lower heat slightly.)

Remove from the oven and cool for 20 minutes. Serve with cream. Serves 6–8.

SHORTCRUST PASTRY

4 cups plain (all-purpose) flour
1/2 cup icing (confectioners') sugar
a pinch of salt

360 g (11 3/4 oz) unsalted butter, cubed
1/2 cup (4 fl oz) cream

Place flour, sifted sugar and salt in a bowl. Add butter and rub through the fingertips until the mixture resembles coarse breadcrumbs. Add just enough cream for mixture to form a ball.

Divide pastry into two balls and wrap separately in plastic wrap. Refrigerate for 30 minutes before using.

Heat the chocolate gently to avoid burning it. Using a metal spoon to fold in the egg whites preserves the air bubbles which make the mousse light and fluffy.

CHOCOLATE MOUSSE

Mousse was the last word when Sydney hadn't learned to poke fun at fondue, and Neil Diamond sang Hot August Night year-round in the 'burbs. Mousse is still doing encores.

450 g (14 oz) good-quality dark chocolate, in small pieces
25 ml (3/4 fl oz) brandy
5 egg whites
4 egg yolks
300 ml (10 fl oz) cream, whipped

Place the chocolate, brandy and 50 ml (13/4 fl oz)of water in a heatproof bowl over a saucepan of hot water. Place over low heat and warm until chocolate has melted. Leave to cool for 5 minutes.

In a small clean dry bowl, beat egg whites until stiff peaks form.

Add egg yolks to chocolate mixture one at a time, beating well after each addition. Fold cream into chocolate mixture and then fold in egg white in two batches, using a large metal spoon.

Pour chocolate mousse into serving bowls or glasses and refrigerate until set. Serves 8.

Try pouring a capful of
Campari over the sorbet just
before serving – for a sunset
effect and bittersweet flavour.

GRAPEFRUIT SORBET WITH ORANGE SALAD

When it's too hot to touch and frangipani petals are melting into the pavement, citrus refreshes lolling tongues. Sorbet slips soothingly down to cool you to the core.

250 g (8 oz) sugar
3 cups (24 fl oz) of strained grapefruit
   juice (about 6 grapefruit)
2 egg whites

to serve
orange salad (below)

Place sugar in a saucepan with 875 ml (28 fl oz) of water over high heat and boil for 5 minutes. Add grapefruit juice and return to the boil. Remove from the heat immediately and cool.

Pour into a shallow metal tray and freeze for 1 hour. Remove from freezer, put into a large bowl and beat until smooth. Return to freezer and repeat the freezing and beating twice more.

Place egg whites in a clean dry bowl and beat until soft peaks form. Remove sorbet from freezer and fold in egg whites. Freeze for a further hour and serve with orange salad. Serves 6.

ORANGE SALAD

6 blood oranges, when in season, or 5 large oranges
juice of 2 oranges
a few drops orange flower water (optional)
10 mint leaves to serve

Peel the oranges, being careful to remove all the pith. Slice oranges horizontally and place in a serving dish. Pour over orange juice and orange flower water, cover and refrigerate for at least an hour.

Remove from refrigerator and scatter with mint leaves. Serve with sorbet.

INDIVIDUAL BLACKBERRY CRUMBLES

Resolve dissolves (crumbles, in fact), when presented with this simple pleasure. Blackberries are best picked from the brambly vine or ranks of punnets in early autumn.

3 cups blackberries

2 tablespoons caster (superfine) sugar

1 cup plain (all-purpose) flour
   plus 1 tablespoon

1/2 cup firmly-packed brown sugar

1 teaspoon baking powder

3 tablespoons quick-cooking oats

100 g (3 1/3 oz) unsalted butter, in small pieces

to serve

vanilla ice cream

Preheat oven to 200°C (400°F). Place the blackberries, caster sugar and the 1 tablespoon of flour in a bowl and toss well to combine.

Place sugar, baking powder, oats and remaining flour in a bowl and mix well. Add butter, and rub in with your fingertips until mixture resembles coarse breadcrumbs. Divide blackberries into two ovenproof bowls, and top with crumble mixture. Bake for 20–25 minutes, until golden brown and bubbling. Serve warm, with ice cream. Serves 2.

For individual pavlovas, make 8 separate mounds on the baking tray and bake for 25–30 minutes.

PAVLOVA

Pavlova recalls childhood memories of extended-family get togethers. It was always baked by an aunt, who would say it wasn't as good as the last one she made. Because she never gave you the recipe, I thought I'd include it.

6 egg whites
1/4 teaspoon cream of tartar
1 teaspoon vanilla essence
1 1/3 cups caster (superfine) sugar
1 tablespoon cornflour (cornstarch)
2 tablespoons arrowroot
2 teaspoons white vinegar

to serve
300 ml (10 fl oz) cream, whipped
pulp of 8 passionfruit

Preheat oven to 220°C (425°F). Place egg whites, cream of tartar and vanilla into a clean dry bowl and beat until stiff peaks form. Add sugar in tablespoons, beating continuously until all sugar is added and meringue is glossy and thick. Stir in the cornflour, arrowroot and vinegar.

Pile onto a baking tray lined with baking paper, in a circle approximately 20 cm (8 in) in diameter.

Turn oven to 150°C (300°F) and bake pavlova for 1 hour 20 minutes, or until the outside is firm but not browned.

Remove from oven and allow to cool completely before serving. Top with whipped cream and passionfruit pulp. Serves 8.

COCONUT RICE PUDDING WITH
PAPAYA AND LIME

Papaya and lime juice reminds so many of us of holidays in Asia. Papaya is the smaller, red-fleshed fruit, quite different in flavour from the large orange-coloured paw-paw.

1/4 cup short-grain rice

1 cup (8 fl oz) coconut milk

100 ml (3 1/3 fl oz) milk

1 teaspoon orange zest

2 tablespoons caster (superfine) sugar

1 teaspoon vanilla essence

100 ml (3 1/3 fl oz) cream

to serve

papaya, peeled, seeded
  and cubed

2 teaspoons brown sugar

lime wedges

Place rice, coconut milk, milk, zest, sugar and vanilla in a saucepan over medium heat, and bring to the boil. Reduce heat immediately to very low. Place a lid on the saucepan and cook for 1 hour, stirring occasionally. When the rice is cooked, remove from heat and leave to cool with the lid on.

When the mixture is cold, stir in cream. Pour into a serving bowl, cover and refrigerate. When ready to serve, remove from the fridge, top with papaya cubes and sprinkle with brown sugar. Serve with wedges of lime on the side. Serves 2.

CHOCOLATE AND RASPBERRY TARTS

At bills, clean healthy flavours tend to rule the entrée and main course menus so there's room for indulgence in desserts. This recipe relies on the tartness of summer berries to offset bittersweet chocolate.

1/2 quantity sweet shortcrust pastry (see page 123)
125 g (4 oz) unsalted butter
200 g (6 1/2 oz) good-quality dark chocolate
2 egg yolks
2 eggs
30 g (1 oz) caster (superfine) sugar
1 1/2 cups raspberries
whipped cream to serve

Divide pastry into four portions and roll each piece out on a lightly floured surface until 3 mm (1/4 in) thick. Press pastry lightly into four individual tart tins and freeze for 30 minutes. Preheat oven to 180°C (350°F).

Line pastry shells with baking paper and baking weights or rice. Bake for 10 minutes. Remove paper and weights and bake for a further 10 minutes, or until pastry is golden, crisp and thoroughly cooked. Allow to cool on wire racks.

Increase oven temperature to 190°C (375°F).

Place butter and chocolate in a heatproof bowl over a saucepan of hot water over low heat and warm until both have melted. Stir, remove from heat and allow to cool for 5 minutes.

Place egg yolks, eggs and sugar in a bowl and beat until thick and creamy. Add the chocolate mixture and mix well. Pour into pastry cases.

Bake tarts for 5 minutes. Remove from oven and arrange raspberries on top of the tarts.

Leave to cool and serve with whipped cream. Serves 4.

dinner | sweet things

BAKED PEACHES WITH VANILLA ICE CREAM AND CARAMEL SAUCE

Peaches blush around the time that summer starts to heat up, but there are still nights when a warm dessert triumphs over fresh fruit. Sugar and baking intensify fruit flavours.

4 peaches, sliced in half,
   stones removed
2 tablespoons brown sugar

to serve
vanilla ice cream
caramel sauce (below)

Preheat the oven to 220°C (425°F). Place peaches, cut-side-up, in a small baking dish and sprinkle with sugar. Bake for 15 minutes, until they are soft and the juices are bubbling. Remove from the oven and cool slightly.

Place peaches in serving dishes, top with vanilla ice cream and pour over caramel sauce. Serves 4.

CARAMEL SAUCE

3/4 cup sugar
3/4 cup (6 fl oz) cream
1 teaspoon lemon juice

Fill the sink with cold water. Place the sugar and a 1/4 cup (2 fl oz) water in a saucepan over low heat and stir until sugar has melted, brushing down the sides of the pan with a clean pastry brush dipped in water if any crystals appear.

Bring to the boil and cook, without stirring, until the caramel turns golden brown, swirling the pan to keep the colour of the caramel even. Remove from the heat as soon as this has occurred, and plunge the base of the pan into the sink of cold water to stop cooking.

Once the caramel has cooled slightly, carefully pour in the cream (it will foam up). When the foaming stops, add the lemon juice and stir until the sauce is smooth. Serve warm.

note To reheat this sauce, place in a saucepan and melt over low heat.

GINGER ICE CREAM WITH CHOCOLATE SAUCE

Ginger in syrup is a fetish, a guilty secret, a temperature-raising sweet treat slurped from sticky jars at midnight. Add it to ice cream and anything can happen.

1/2 cup sugar
1 cup (8 fl oz) milk
1 cup (8 fl oz) cream
4 egg yolks
3 tablespoons drained
   preserved ginger in syrup,
   cut into small pieces

to serve
chocolate sauce (below)

Place sugar, milk and cream in a saucepan over medium heat, and stir the mixture occasionally, until it is scalded and the sugar dissolved.

Place egg yolks in a bowl and beat until light and thick. Gradually add hot milk mixture, beating constantly. Return mixture to a clean saucepan and stir over a medium-low heat, without boiling, until custard has thickened. Remove from heat, stir in ginger and leave to cool completely. Pour into an ice cream maker and follow manufacturer's instructions. Serve with chocolate sauce. Makes 6.

CHOCOLATE SAUCE

125 g (4 oz) good-quality dark chocolate
3/4 cup (6 fl oz) cream

Place chocolate and cream in a heatproof bowl over a saucepan of hot water over medium heat. Whisk occasionally, until a thick sauce forms. Cool slightly and serve with ice cream. Serves 6.

DINNER DRINKS + NIBBLES

As the sun sinks behind the Blue Mountains, Sydneysiders balance a drink, a napkin and something to nibble on with ease. The Asian kitchen adapts a wok-ful of entrée dishes to bring spice to these parties.

DUCK AND BEANSPROUT SPRING ROLLS

1/4 cup (2 fl oz) hoisin sauce

2 tablespoons Chinese black vinegar

1 teaspoon sesame oil

2 teaspoons grated fresh ginger

1 teaspoon orange zest

11/2 cups shredded barbecue duck

24 spring roll wrappers

6 spring (green) onions, cut into 6 cm (21/2 in) lengths

1/2 cup bean sprouts

2 egg whites, lightly beaten

oil for deep frying

Place hoisin sauce, vinegar, sesame oil, ginger and orange zest in a bowl and stir to combine. Combine half this sauce with the shredded duck and mix well.

Lay out 2 spring roll wrappers at a time, on top of each other so that they form a double layer. Place 1 heaped tablespoon of duck mixture evenly across one corner of each double spring roll wrapper, and add a piece of spring onion and a few bean sprouts. Brush edges with beaten egg whites and roll up tightly, folding in the sides so that the filling is completely enclosed.

Heat oil in a heavy frying pan or wok until hot. Shallow-fry rolls a few at a time until golden. Remove and drain on paper towels while cooking the rest. Serve with the remaining hoisin sauce for dipping. Makes 12.

WHITE PEACH AND MANGO FRAPPÉ

1 tablespoon caster (superfine) sugar

2 tablespoons boiling water

1 cup ice

1/2 cup chopped mango

1/2 cup chopped white peach

1 teaspoon lime juice

100 ml (31/3 fl oz) white rum

Dissolve the sugar in the boiling water to make a syrup. Place in a blender with the remaining ingredients and blend until smooth. Serves 1 in a large glass.

SPRING ONION BREAD

2 cups plain (all-purpose) flour
2 teaspoons baking powder
3 teaspoons sea salt
3/4–1 cup (6–8 fl oz) boiling water
2 tablespoons vegetable oil
1 tablespoon chilli oil
1 tablespoon sesame oil
4 spring (green) onions, finely sliced
vegetable oil for frying

Place flour, baking powder and 1 teaspoon sea salt in a food processor. Add boiling water in a thin stream and process until dough forms a ball. (The amount of water needed will depend on the flour used.)

Remove dough from food processor to a board and knead for 2 minutes, using extra flour if dough sticks to the board. Wrap dough in plastic wrap and allow to rest for at least 30 minutes.

Divide dough into six equal pieces and roll each portion on a lightly floured surface until 25 cm (10 in) in diameter. Combine the three kinds of oil in a bowl and brush some on the dough. Sprinkle each dough circle with 1/4 teaspoon of salt and 2 teaspoons of spring onions. Roll bread, swiss-roll fashion, and then coil up. Roll out again into circles 15 cm (6 in) in diameter.

Heat a non-stick frying pan (with lid) over medium heat and add 3 tablespoons of oil. Add bread, cover the pan and reduce heat to low. After 3 minutes check the bread: if it is golden brown underneath, turn and cook the other side; if not, cook for another minute and check again.

When the bread is golden brown on both sides, remove from pan and drain on paper towels. Cook the remaining 5 rounds of dough. Cut each round into six pieces and sprinkle with sea salt. Makes 36 slices.

FRESH LIME JUICE AND VODKA

1 tablespoon caster (superfine) sugar
2 tablespoons boiling water
50 ml (1 3/4 fl oz) vodka
2 tablespoons lime juice

4 lime leaves
ice
soda water

Dissolve the sugar in the boiling water and cool. Divide vodka, lime juice, lime leaves (two per glass), sugar syrup and ice between 2 glasses and top with soda water. Serves 2.

BILL'S FAVOURITES

AC Butchery
Great handmade sausages and organic meats
174 Marion Street, Leichhardt.
Tel: 9569 8687

A & P Sulfaro
Gelati and bread
119 Ramsay Road, Haberfield.
Tel: 9797 0001

Billy Kwong
Shop 3, 355 Crown Street, Surry Hills.
Tel: 9332 3300

bills
433 Liverpool Street, Darlinghurst.
Tel: 9360 9631

bills2
359 Crown Street, Surry Hills.
Tel: 9360 4762

Emperors Garden BBQ and Noodles
Terrific Chinese barbecued meats
213 Thomas Street, Haymarket.
Tel: 9281 9899

Haberfield Bakery
The best wood-fired bread
153 Ramsay Road, Haberfield.
Tel: 9797 7715

Herbies Spices
Dried spices with oomph
745 Darling Street, Rozelle.
Tel: 9555 6035

La Passion du Fruit
Tingling fruit frappés
633 Bourke Street, Surry Hills.
Tel: 9690 1894

MFC Supermarket Mascot
For Lebanese spices, sweets and variety of olives
455 Gardeners Road, Mascot.
Tel: 9669 6136.

Mohr Food
Superb smoked fish, especially gravlax
4 Luff Street, Botany. Tel: 9316 6126

Northern Chinese Noodle Restaurant
Handmade dumplings and noodles
Shop 7, Burlington Centre, Cnr Quay
and Thomas Streets, Haymarket.
Tel: 9281 9051

Paesanella
The freshest ricotta and mozzarella
27 Gerald Street, Marrickville.
Tel: 9519 6181

Pastabilities
A wide variety of fresh pasta and inventive sauces
45 Albion Street, Surry Hills.
Tel: 9281 0267

Pasticceria Papa
Mouthwatering pastries allsorts
145 Ramsay Road, Haberfield.
Tel: 9798 6894

Pontip
An Asian supermarket with a Thai emphasis
445 Pitt Street, Haymarket.
Tel: 9211 2208

Quinton's Artisan Bakery
For pastry snails and crusty breads to fuel walks
179 The Mall, Leura (Blue Mountains).
Tel: 02 4784 1880

Sydney Fishmarket
Pyrmont Bridge Road, Pyrmont.
Tel: 9660 1611

Sydney Morning Herald Good
Living Growers Market
Pyrmont Bay Park, Pyrmont.

Thai-Kee Supermarket
Great Asian supermarket for one-stop shopping
393 Sussex Street, Sydney.
Tel: 9281 2202

ONE-STOP SHOPS

David Jones Food Hall
Cnr Market and
Castlereagh Streets
Sydney.
Tel: 9266 5544

Fuel Food
490 Crown Street,
Surry Hills.
Tel: 9383 9399

GPO
GPO Building,
Cnr George Street and
Martin Place,
Sydney.
Tel: 9229 7704

Jones the Grocer
68 Moncur Street,
Woollahra.
Tel: 9362 1222
36 Campbell Parade,
Bondi.
Tel: 9130 1100

Simon Johnson Purveyor
of Quality Foods
181 Harris Street,
Pyrmont.
Tel: 9552 2522
55 Queen St,
Woollahra.
Tel: 9328 6888

* Bacon 2.50   * Roast tom
* Mushrooms 2.50 * Fresh tom
          * Ricotta H

* Sweetcorn fritter
(½ portions

INDEX

          * Spring o
          Spinach
    * Seared Salmon
          Asian
* Goats cheese and Bab
    * Prawn + chilli

CONVERSION CHART
1 cup = 250 ml (8 fl oz)
1 Australian tablespoon = 20 ml
1 UK tablespoon = 15 ml
1 teaspoon = 5 ml